Movement Variability in Soccer Training

T0355821

DIOGO COUTINHO • SARA SANTOS • JAIME SAMPAIO

MOVEMENT VARIABILITY
in Soccer Training

Enrich Your Training Sessions to Enhance and Develop Player Creativity

Meyer & Meyer Sport

British Library of Cataloguing in Publication Data

A catalogue record for this book is available from the British Library

Movement Variability in Soccer Training
Maidenhead: Meyer & Meyer Sport (UK) Ltd., 2024
ISBN: 978-1-78255-254-3

© 2024 by Meyer & Meyer Sport (UK) Ltd.
Aachen, Auckland, Beirut, Cairo, Cape Town, Dubai, Hägendorf, Hong Kong, Indianapolis, Maidenhead, Manila, New Delhi, Singapore, Sydney, Tehran, Vienna

Member of the World Sport Publishers' Association (WSPA), www.w-s-p-a.org
Printed by Print Consult GmbH, Munich, Germany
Printed in Slovakia

ISBN: 978-1-78255-254-3
Email: info@m-m-sports.com
www.thesportspublisher.com

Contents

Foreword

Releasing the potential in all of our children must be the goal for every parent, coach, or volunteer. In addition, we must strive to develop, within each child, a lifelong love of playing sport and being physically active. Feeling confident about your ability to participate is the first important step, so the development of a robust, varied, and skilled movement capability is vital.

Each page of this book will help coaches understand how to plan, implement, and reflect upon their development programs in order to maximize returns in the domains of movement variability, the fostering of creativity, and, most importantly, the promotion of new learning. The sheer randomness of the game of soccer requires high levels of adaptability both in perception action as well as in the player's physical responses.

The millions of fans who watch the game are also desperate to be entertained. Creative players will solve those situations in the game with novel and unexpected responses. This capability can be enhanced, and the book outlines a methodology for the creation of enriched environments that nurture the player's divergent thinking and motor skills.

This book has influenced my work in such a positive way, and I would recommend it to anyone who is involved in education, sports coaching, and the development of young people. It skillfully presents a combination of relevant research supplemented by lots of practical examples to help deepen the understanding of such an important area.

–Peter Sturgess
The Football Association

Preface

Sharing knowledge is always an act of generosity, and this book is a good example of that. As a neighbor of this community of "facilitators" who cohabit this wonderful world that is training football, I thank Sara, Diogo, and Jaime for their invaluable contribution through this work, and for all the (many) research that have inspired us day by day to help these players with whom we are lucky to share, as Professor Paco Seirul-lo would say, this (in)formative journey.

Based on the need to practice with our athletes under the paradigm of complexity, the practice in variability that the authors propose in this work allows us to manage this necessary continuous modification of contexts in order to facilitate the adaptation of our players to them, thus causing the emergence of flexible behaviors away from modelling, stereotyped responses, and rigid motor solutions, really suboptimal in a sport with a high level of uncertainty such as the one we are dealing with.

The recommendation of the use of exploratory tasks, which the authors share with us, constitutes an efficient invitation to adaptability from the practice in variability, which will therefore allow the cultivation of individual and collective creativity, key to the optimization of the "playing" of our athletes, thus emerging new attractors or making others that have already emerged previously more flexible. Jaime, Sara, and Diogo, with their proposal, propose to avoid the excessive stabilization of some attractors that, without this variable practice, would limit the possibilities of exploration of our players in relation to possible new actions and emerging interactions during the game.

Reading these pages, the need to flee from pre-established models will grow within us, bringing us closer to adopting a role, as technical trainers, more based on facilitation than on direction, on the enhancement of implicit learning, within a context of variety, which favors the emancipation of the player within the game. The reflections shared by the three authors in this text can help us to change the intervention of the player for the exchange, turning our contribution to the athlete into something more efficient than sensationalist.

We are talking about a sincere approach to the natural expression of the athlete in favor of that longed-for autonomy of the player. In the same way that in a rondo we can consider as a strategy to "condition" the game to a contact with the object that different motor actions emerge, perhaps creative, understanding this conditioning or constraint as a disturbance that seeks to destabilize the player but in no case tries to improve "the game to a contact," the authors of this work invite us to reflect on the important role that variability has in the adoption of (in)finite registers to be adopted by the athletes in the framework of the optimization of their decision-making system. Jorge Wagensberg from Barcelona used to say, "the lung needs air, the heart needs blood and the mouth needs saliva, [but] the brain needs change," and this is exactly what the authors offer their athletes through variable practices such as those expressed in these lines that we can read below, applying Mayer's principle of turning "the game itself into its master." This variability will lead the player to optimize his creativity, a concept that the authors avoid, rightly in my opinion, attributing to the innate capacity of the athlete, understanding that this creativity can be "trained" as long as a context is offered that allows for "divergent discovery." In this practice space, the player will find his own challenges from, for example, constraints proposed by the coach, and will end up driving the ball, passing it or shooting it at goal with the intention of being efficient, without being subjected to inductive exchanges by the coach.

On more than one occasion, I have heard one of the authors of the book, Jaime Sampaio, say that, "the way we configure the environment is the way in which we will later ask our players for answers," and this work that we have in our hands today will help us to generate that context which does not intend to induce specific movement behaviors in the athletes, but rather contribute to their recalling old and developing new movement patterns according to specific coordination and tactical requirements that the players will consider appropriate for a unique and unrepeatable moment. These movement patterns will be grounded according to their capabilities, potential, naturalized behaviors, emotions... their resources. As Juanma Lillo says, "in a match we see what we know, not what is happening."

We could understand this text as a manual for disturbing the athlete, as long as we have internalized beforehand that practice in variability does not expose the team to the "danger" of "training mistakes" but rather is about inviting the players to a series of adaptations according to an intentionally designed environment. In the endless and wonderful exchanges I have daily with my colleagues in the Methodology Department at FC Barcelona, in which the authors of this book have participated directly or indirectly on more than one occasion, a reflection has frequently appeared that connects with the feeling that underlies this text: From the linear perspective, to train an error is to do something that does not reproduce the "real conditions of the game," but this vision of practice will invite the perpetuation of the previously mentioned pre-established models, when "training errors" under our paradigm would be not respecting the external focus, the player's flow, especially in the initial training of the football player, it will be necessary to understand this game of football beyond the normative, seeking to offer these young athletes a space of continuous exploration based on generic concepts of the game such as space/time, teammates/opponents, directionality, trajectories...

If we change the perspective from modelling to disturbing, we will see that it is an opportunity for the player to self-organize in search of a main intention (specific to each game idea), avoiding that common underestimation existing in many training proposals towards the adaptive capacity of the human being athlete.

–Isaac Guerrero
Deputy Director of the Methodology Department at FC Barcelona

Acknowledgments

The authors would like to express their sincere thanks to all involved people in this book. From the players who engaged in the sessions to the people that capture their performances through video and photograph as well as to those who directly or indirectly participated in bringing it to life. It was a privilege to work with such talented and amazing people.

Introduction

This book provides a practical perspective on how additional variability can complement soccer training drills. To fulfill this purpose, the first section of the book offers a brief general theoretical background supporting the benefits of adding movement variability, and the second section contains 90 training tasks that are divided into four task types: (1) nano-level tasks, which are tasks without opposition, focus on challenging the players to explore and create new movement patterns; (2) micro-level (individual-based) tasks consist of game-based situations that face low opposition levels (e.g., 1vs1, 1vs1+4 neutral players); (3) meso-level tasks (group-based) focus on developing cooperative and competitive tendencies between teams with low tactical complexity; and (4) macro-level tasks (collective-based) are embodied in a high tactical complexity and emphasize more positioning-based solutions. These tasks were created with additional variability, and progressions have been added to assist all readers in using, adapting, and creating their own training sessions.

Part I: Developing Enriched Learning Environments

Part I presents the theoretical background in support of movement variability. The information presented in this section acts as a key precursor for acquiring novel behaviors and is fundamental to developing a better understanding of the tasks created in Part II.

Chapter 1: The Nature of Soccer

This chapter characterizes soccer from a functional and structural perspective, emphasizing how the available information about the environment guides players' movement behaviors. From this viewpoint, it also describes how varying task constraints emphasize different information and, consequently, afford different opportunities for action. Finally, this chapter discusses players' performance using four scales of analysis (nano, micro, meso, and macro), which support the design and division of the training task categories.

Chapter 2: The Rise of Creativity

This chapter explores the importance of creativity in developing a soccer player's expert performance. In this regard, this chapter contextualizes the developmental trends of creativity, presents a comprehensive framework intended to nurture creative enriching environments during the early years, and discusses the factors that affect the process of developing creativity. This chapter also emphasizes pedagogical perspectives and guidelines that coaches should incorporate when designing training tasks, mainly based on movement variability, to create an enriching and supportive environment for creativity to thrive.

Chapter 3: The Role of Variability in Performance and Learning

This chapter presents general perspectives on movement variability and moves toward a more practical perspective. In this chapter, readers will acknowledge the benchmarks of adding movement variability and learn how to include variability in the training tasks to ensure a more effective acquisition of new movement skills. Ultimately, the main results regarding the acute and chronic effects of adding variability during training practices in soccer will be presented, ranging from analytical to more game-based tasks.

Part II: Designing Training Tasks

Part II presents 90 training tasks embedded in variability according to four main themes: nano-level tasks, micro-level tasks, meso-level tasks, and macro-level tasks. This categorization enables readers to better follow the main aim of each category and better understand how to integrate variability into the corresponding session aims.

Chapter 4: Adding Variability

The chapter starts with a brief explanation of the concepts and primary principles that compose the nano, micro, meso, and macro scales before presenting and describing 90 training tasks with additional variability.

Chapter 5: Periodization of Variability

This chapter proposes the periodization of variability in regard to the four main categories, exemplifying a way for players to identify opportunities that will enhance their soccer performance. This chapter also takes into consideration soccer players' individualities and competition demands and therefore highlights the need for developing training designs that require high variability and adaptability.

PART I

Developing Enriched Learning Environments

CHAPTER 1

The Nature of Soccer

Soccer is an invasion team sport in which the team in possession aims to progress down the field toward the goal and create goal scoring opportunities, while the team without possession looks to stay compact and restrict the available space, intending to protect their goal and recover possession of the ball (Grehaigne et al., 1997). Two opposing teams, each composed of eleven players (including the goalkeeper), compete in space and time to gain an advantage over their opponents. In the search for this space, players develop cooperative and competitive interactions with their teammates and opponents (McGarry et al., 2002). For example, the team in possession attempts to use the entire pitch space to attack and increase their distance from the nearest defender, allowing more time to decide how best to perform. The defending team stays compact and attempts to put pressure on the opponent with the ball by decreasing the available space (i.e., prevent player progression in the pitch) and time to restrict the possibility of the player in possession of the ball in exploring the best offensive options (e.g., passing and dribbling). The players from the same team must work together to develop functionally collective behaviors that allow them to pursue a collective goal, while at the same time competing with the opponents in search of spatial and temporal dominance (Grehaigne et al., 1997; Passos et al., 2016).

Performance in soccer results from a continuous process of co-adaptation between the players and teams in the search for functional movement behaviors (Araujo & Davids, 2016; Araújo et al., 2006; Passos et al., 2016). That is, the players belonging to one team will adjust their behavior in relation to their individual characteristics; for example, if the left fullback is a player characterized by lower displacement speed and faces a technically developed (1vs1 skills) winger who possesses high sprinting ability, the team may be positioned closer to the left corridor when defending. Similarly, while attacking, if the defending team retreats close to their target, this may imply that the offensive team explores more of the lateral spaces of the pitch to destabilize the defensive team (co-adaptation in the search for functional behaviors). Based on these assumptions, performance has been conceived and analyzed from the perspective of how players adjust their movement behavior according to the various configurations of play (Folgado et al., 2014) and to changes in the environment (Travassos et al., 2012a). That is, players coordinate their actions in space and time with their teammates according to the available information, such as the distance to target (Vilar et al., 2014), distance to teammates (Gonçalves et al., 2014), and their position in relation to the ball position (Gonçalves et al., 2019). For example, after losing the ball that led to a 3vs2+Gk defensive situation, the defending players may retreat to their own goal in an attempt to gain time that will allow more teammates to recover while also putting pressure on the player in possession in the penalty area to limit possible attempts to score. Under this example, players adjust their positioning according to local numerical relations (3vs2) and space (i.e., they retreat when close to the defensive half and press forward when close to their goal). Therefore, the players' positioning on the pitch is a reflection of how each individual player explores the environmental information to support their actions (Gonçalves et al., 2016; Seifert et al., 2013; Travassos et al., 2012a). This evidence highlights that different functional behaviors emerge as a consequence of the players' abilities to interact with the surrounding environment.

Players should be able to interpret the available environment and be independent and confident in being different and adaptive.

Perception and Action

The environment acts as a key role in the players' decision since it contains informational properties that the players use to aid their decisions (Araújo et al., 2006; Fajen, 2007; Le Runigo et al., 2005; Travassos et al., 2012a). In this regard, player and team performances are based on the performer-environment relationship, in which the players support their actions according to the available information (Gibson, 1986). That is, opportunities to act (i.e., affordances) will emerge as the performers move and interact with the environmental information to support the emergence of goal-directed behaviors (Fajen, 2005; Fajen et al., 2009). For example, when two players are playing on the street, and suddenly, one kicks the ball and it stays trapped in a tree. To retrieve the ball, the players will explore the environment: If the tree is easy to climb, they may be able to retrieve it themselves; otherwise, they may search for other solutions, such as searching for a chair that might help them to increase their height or asking an adult to assist them. In this case, the adult opportunities for action would be different from those of the kids because, since the adult is likely taller, he may be able to retrieve the ball without needing to search for other materials to help increase his size. Under this scope, two different types of affordances can be considered: (1) body-scaled affordances, which refer to individual action capabilities, such as the ability of a defender to jump to cut the ball, and (2) action-scaled affordances, which relate to environmental properties, such as when the movement of a teammate opens space (i.e., the diagonal movement of a forward that attracts the opposing defender to move with him) for the player in possession to explore (Fajen et al., 2009). In general, the players' ability to act (e.g., power, physical skills, motivation, tactical awareness, and individual constraints) and the environmental information (e.g., movement of teammates and opponents) will guide players' movement behaviors. For example, when performing a dribble, the player in possession analyzes the defender's body orientation and the available space to decide how to successfully dribble around the opponent. The player retrieves information, such as the perceived distance to the nearest defender, by reading his body orientation to provoke misalignments (Duarte et al., 2012) and identifies the available space based on the distance from the other defenders to the goal and to the pitch boundaries (Coutinho et al., 2020). However, because of the dynamic nature of soccer, the opportunities for action appear and disappear continuously based on the spatial-temporal interactions that emerge between the teammates and direct opponents (Le Runigo et al., 2005; Passos et al., 2016; Travassos et al., 2012a). Using the previous example, if the player in possession holds the ball for a long time without exploring different changes in speed and direction, it may be possible that the distance to the nearest defender decreases in such a way that would not allow the player to overcome the defender in the available space. As these examples show, players couple their actions, both in space and time, with the information, allowing them to decide when and how to perform (Le Runigo et al., 2005). Therefore, players' movement behaviors in the pitch will depend upon their ability to exploit, identify, and use the relevant information in the competitive environment (Araújo et al., 2006; Fajen et al., 2009). Taking these findings into consideration, players must be challenged to refine their perceptual-action systems by exposing them to training tasks that help to develop their understanding of which actions are possible according to the environment and each individual's action capabilities (Fajen, 2007).

"The best teachers are those who show you where to look, but don't tell you what to see."

–Alexandra Trenfor

Constraints Shape Players' Decisions

The constraints-led approach consists of a theoretical approach underpinned in dynamical systems, ecological psychology, and non-linear pedagogy that characterize players as open systems, which implies a mutual relationship between the performer and the surrounding environment (Renshaw et al., 2019). As exemplified earlier, players will interact with the environment to solve their problems (e.g., retrieve the ball from the tree). Constraints create boundary conditions that shape and guide the players' movement behaviors. According to Newell (1986a), the constraints can be classified according to three types: (1) environmental constraints, which concern the physical and social proprieties of the surrounding environment, such as the weather, light conditions, altitude (physical-related factors), and even the support from the group of peers and cultural expectations (social factors); (2) individual constraints, which reflect the performer's individual characteristics, such as motivation, cognitive skills, and height; and (3) task constraints, which relate to manipulations in the task, such as the pitch size, number of players, game rules, or type of materials included. For example, the way a team presses the opposing team's goal kick will depend on the match status (e.g., if the team is losing, it is more likely to press [task constraint]), the individual players' ability to press (e.g., motivation, level of endurance [individual constraints]), or even the type of weather (e.g., during windy conditions, the last line is more likely to stay closer to their goal as a result of the no offside rule during the goal kick [environmental constraints]).

These constraints all provide information about the performers, which they use to regulate their actions (Fajen, 2005; Fajen, 2007). In fact, players' actions emerge as a result of temporary couplings between the individual and the environment (Chow et al., 2015; Davids et al., 2008; Newell, 1986b). As such, the constraints provide the space in which the players act, allowing them to explore a certain number of action possibilities according to each individual's ability (Newell et al., 2003; Orth et al., 2017). For example, a player may have to adjust the tension applied to the ball when playing on a wet pitch compared to a dry pitch (physical environmental-related constraint). In the same way, a defender may adjust his distance to the direct opponent when in possession (e.g., a fullback facing a winger) according to his individual characteristics, such as speed, power, and technical ability (individual constraints).

Each player has their own action capabilities. That is, the solution that best suits one player may not necessarily be the best solution for another player, even when facing a similar condition. For example, while one player may be able to shoot at the target during a free kick from a long distance, another player may not be able to shoot from such a distance, and crossing the ball might emerge as the most effective solution. Regarding the task constraints, the players may adjust their positioning on the pitch according to their perception of information derived from the task. For example, players may increase the pressure on the opponents when defending a regular-size goal without a goalkeeper to limit the opposing players' opportunities to shoot; however, they will defend close to the goal when protecting many small targets because of the higher number of possibilities for the opposing team to score (Travassos et al., 2014). Therefore, all types of constraints provide information to the players that leads them to adjust their movement behaviors; however, the individual and task constraints are most relevant for coaches, as those are the types of constraints that can be manipulated by coaches (Renshaw et al., 2010).

Based on previous findings, it is important that coaches design training tasks that encourage players to be fine-tuned to the environmental information. To achieve such an aim, coaches should account for three essential concepts: (1) the representativeness of training, (2) the stability and instability during training sessions, and (3) the level of information complexity (Otte et al., 2019; Otte et al., 2020). The representativeness of training relates to how much of a skill developed during training practices transfers to the match (Pinder et al., 2011; Travassos et al., 2012b). To create representative learning environments, coaches must design tasks that maintain a similar perceptual-motor landscape as the one players face during the competition (Travassos et al., 2012b).

Using the previous example of the dribbling action, to successfully dribble around an opponent, the player in possession uses information from the body of the defender and the available space to decide what to do; it is important to maintain this information when aiming to develop the dribbling skill. A proper understanding of the creation of representative environments can be seen in the work of Farrow and Robertson (2017), where the authors propose an equation that guides coaches to recognize the transfer between training and a match.

The second concept, stability and instability, is of paramount importance for training, as movement stability allows players to maintain a structure for their performance, while instability produces fluctuations that contribute to the emergence of functional and adaptable movement patterns (Otte et al., 2019; Otte et al., 2020; Seifert et al., 2013). To achieve these intentions, coaches must create training tasks that lead players to perform the same movement under different patterns (Buszard et al., 2017). In fact, this instability will prevent players from experiencing training monotony and a state of tedium that can develop from being bored by the absence of non-variable practices (Farrow & Robertson, 2017). A continuum of variety can be added during training practices to maximize the development of adaptive movement behaviors (Farrow & Robertson, 2017), which can be achieved by adding variability during a particular single session or by adding it from a longitudinal viewpoint. (For more details, see the periodization section in chapter 5.)

Lastly, the level of information complexity, which relates to the task information complexity, consists of the amount of information a player should acquire to perform successfully (Otte et al., 2019; Otte et al., 2020). As such, coaches may amplify or decrease the perceptual demands of the player to manipulate the available affordances for a given task (Davids, 2014; Otte et al., 2019; Otte et al., 2020). For example, coaches may add a pitch corridor and sectorial lines (increasing the amount of available information) to amplify information about the use of space (i.e., team dispersion) (Coutinho et al., 2019) [36]. It is also important to note that task informational complexity may vary between individuals during the same task (e.g., during a rondo 6+1vs3, the player in the middle acting as a neutral player will face more perceptual demands compared to the players staying outside and in possession).

Coaches should make room for exploration, mistakes, risk taking, and open mindedness, and should not expect instant results.

Different Scales of Analysis

The players' performance largely depends on their ability to capture the information that is available within the environment and determine how the individual and spatiotemporal constraints allow them to perform with the influence of previous strategic decisions and local adaptations (Sampaio et al., 2019). From this viewpoint, different levels of analysis can be considered when designing training tasks to improve players' performance.

At the nano level, the players are exposed to more analytic-based training tasks (i.e., without cooperation or opposition) to prepare them for scenarios of higher uncertainty that require individual adaptability. At the micro level, the opposition starts to emerge (e.g., 1vs1 situations), and the players should embrace the nano performance acquired at the previous level. Several studies have explored the factors linked with attacker or defender success (Duarte et al., 2012; Grehaigne et al., 1997; Laakso et al., 2017) at this level and addressed the interpersonal coordination tendencies between the attacker and the defender in relation to their distance, the distance to the goal, or the individual and relative velocity (i.e., the difference between the attacker's and defender's speed). At the meso level, cooperation is added in as a key factor and includes cooperation and opposition interactions sustained with less complexity compared to formal matches. At this level of analysis, the focus relates to exploring the cooperative and competitive tendencies that emerge between players and the confronting teams, usually in the format of small-sided games. Several studies have been conducted to determine how players adapt their behavior according to teammates' and opponents' behaviors (Aguiar et al., 2015; Folgado et al., 2019; Gonçalves et al., 2016). Finally, the macro level includes formal game situations, in which it is possible to understand how the team behaves collectively and coordinates their actions. At this level, studies have explored the dynamics of the movement of players and teams, which show more extraordinary levels of movement regularity and predictability (Duarte et al., 2013; Gonçalves et al., 2014). Coaches should therefore take into consideration the different levels of analyses and the information flow at each level when designing training tasks to improve players' performance.

The best teams find the perfect balance between having clear game strategies and allowing players a certain amount of freedom to take individual initiative and display creativity.

CHAPTER 2

The Rise of Creativity

The demand for creativity has received growing interest in distinct domains, such as education, arts, and sports sciences (Runco, 2014). In the past, creativity was typically addressed within the discussion of genius and linked with the divine, and it remained this way until the second half of the twentieth century. The study of creativity was driven by Joy Paul Guilford's influential speech as part of the American Psychology Association (APA) in 1950. Following this statement, Guilford suggested that individuals were able to improve their creative performance and, therefore, it should be measured (Guilford, 1950; Guilford, 1967). As a result, many lines of research have been explored in this vein, including in sports sciences (Becker, 1995; Becker, 2011).

Generally, the concept of creativity has been linked to the production of something novel or rare, which is appropriate and considered valued by society (Kaufman & Baer, 2012; Runco & Jaeger, 2012). Creativity has equally been related to a characteristic of human thinking, reflecting the ability to solve problems in an original way and to produce work that is novel, adequate, and socially recognized (Razumnikova, 2007). Grounded in cognitive science, a common way to define creativity is the ability to produce something which is both new, original, and task and domain appropriate, which relates creativity with the capacity to produce work that is both novel (original and unexpected) and useful (Stenberg & Lubart, 1995; Stenberg & Lubart, 1999). Hence, the criteria for product novelty and appropriateness have long been seen as the hallmark of creativity. Creativity has also been linked to Guilford's definition of divergent thinking, which includes the production of solutions to a particular problem with a focus on variety and quantity, and recent reports have confirmed that it is a reliable and valid predictor to gauge creativity (Runco & Acar, 2012). It is also accepted by the relevant research that convergent thinking plays a meaningful role for the creative predisposition as well. Convergent thinking is considered to generate the most appropriate solution to a given problem and relies on logic, high accuracy, and speed (Cropley, 2006). Nevertheless, the available literature highlights divergent thinking as the mainstream concept of creativity commonly used to assess creative potential in different fields. Usually, divergent thinking encompasses four creative components distinguished as fluency (generate several solutions), versatility (different categories of solutions), elaboration (detailed solutions), and originality (uniqueness of solutions). These components are considered a comprehensive measure of creative potential (Kim, 2006) and have been widely used in tests such as the Torrance Test of Creative Thinking (TTCT), Remotes Associates Test (RAT), and Consensual Assessment Technique (CAT).

The creativity concept evolved from unidimensional to multidimensional perspectives and from factors linked to individual characteristics associated with the environment (Harrington, 2011). This advancement in the conceptualization of creativity has allowed the exploration of its role in sports as well as the development of deeper knowledge in this field to nurture creative behaviors (Santos et al., 2016; Santos et al., 2017). Though the concept of creativity is not concrete and may entail a broader scope of application in soccer (Fardilha & Allen, 2019), creative behavior has been extensively described as an organic process which generates several solutions for solving a game or training problem in a feasible, unexpected, and authentic way under the appropriate environmental conditions (Memmert, 2015b; Santos & Monteiro, 2021). In this regard, creativity should be understood as the process of perceiving, exploring, and generating novel opportunities for action within a given context (Rasmussen et al., 2019). Thus, a more functional, ecological, and relational perspective was proposed as an updated conceptualization. In soccer, creativity has been described as the player's disposition to move under the guidance of the environment and become attuned to the ability to solve a specific game problem in a novel, feasible, unexpected, and original way by starting a single act or flowing in a collective action and contributing to team success (Santos et al., 2016).

A creative predisposition seems to follow distinct patterns across the players' development paths. In fact, while convergent thinking seems to remain stable throughout the players' path, divergent abilities are more likely to decrease when not stimulated (Alfonso-Benlliure et al., 2013). The reason for such differences may be associated with the significant encouragement of convergent thinking during a child's education. This higher focus on convergent behavior during childhood seems to impact their creative potential. Several studies have reported that children's creativity begins to decline around age six, and a *creative slump* occurs in the fourth and six grades (Claxton et al., 2005). To mitigate this slump, it is of paramount importance that teachers and coaches develop proper enrichment environments to nurture children's thinking and motor divergent abilities.

Looking for P-type Creativity During the Early Years

According to Boden's Impossibility Theory to Creativity, to support creative environments, coaches should be aware that two different creative expressions emerge during the developmental process characterized as the P-type (personal creativity) and H-type (historical creativity) creativity types (Boden, 1996). H-type creativity is an action widely recognized as being novel by society; it is an innovative behavior that no player has ever executed before, and it is commonly connected to a high level of expertise (Boden, 1996). In soccer, the novel game behaviors of Ronaldinho, Messi, Ibrahimovic, and Cristiano Ronaldo are an accurate example of H-type creativity. This expression is easier to recognize in sports and is commonly highlighted in creativity conceptualization. P-type creativity is related to the creation of something that is new to the player who performed it but not necessarily to society (see figure 1). This creative expression is internal to the player, and it relates to the self-exploration of new techniques and discovery of solutions that are novel for them, allowing them to overcome personal limitations (Boden, 1996). During the early years, soccer coaches should nurture P-type creativity in their practices by promoting a supportive environment that favors openness to new challenges and a positive development climate to explore new behaviors as well as inspires confidence to engage in unpredictable training tasks. To enact this, it is essential to include in the training practices the four creative components: fluency, versatility (or flexibility), attempts, and originality (Coutinho et al., 2018; Santos et al., 2018; Santos et al., 2017) extensively adapted from Guilford's (1950) classical research.

H-Creativity (historical creativity) - creation of something that no one has ever done.

P-Creativity (personal creativity) - creation of something new to the individual (not to the world).

Figure 1. Examples of H-type (Higuita scorpion kick) and P-type creativity, represented by the first player to perform a new movement action (e.g., roulette).

Creating Enriching and Supportive Environments

Creative coaching is about creating an environment that allows players to feel comfortable using their imagination without fear, leading to originality in performance.

More recently, creative components have become widely used to trigger creative potential in sports (Caso & van der Kamp, 2020; Memmert & Roth, 2007; Santos et al., 2017; Santos & Monteiro, 2020). Accordingly, fluency or efficacy is the ability to execute as many effective movement actions as possible to overcome a game problem. Versatility or flexibility refers to the variety of actions that a player or team are likely to produce, such as exploring different ways to pass (e.g., a back pass from Cristiano Ronaldo). Originality covers the production of novel and rare behavioral solutions, whereas attempts are recognized as any effort to perform a non-standard action (versatile) without success (see Santos et al., 2016). Considering that coaches should view creativity as a developmental process, they should make room for mistakes or inappropriate decisions when cultivating this disposition in soccer. For a novice player, the attempt is of paramount importance to encourage them to explore new ways of performing actions, providing a greater chance that rare interactions emerge (Santos et al., 2016). This preliminary exploratory behavior will provide a foundation for upcoming creative components, such as being able to dribble in an effective way (fluency) and nurture the ability to perform the dribble in unexpected ways (versatility) until they attain a unique dribbling action (originality). These components have also been used to measure a player's creative potential in performance-based situations with regard to task representativeness and ecological validity through the Creative Behavior Assessment in Team Sports (CBATS) (Santos et al., 2016; Santos et al., 2017; Santos et al., 2018).

Coaches should design open-ended tasks that include variability to provide players with a chance to discover personally unique ways to use their abilities.

Currently, coaches face design barriers for creativity, as reported in Rasmussen et al. (2020), which highlighted issues relating to the club's soccer-specific curriculum. The coaching preference was for more prescriptive practices and formal games, and variability was not included in their training tasks. The club was constantly evaluated by external consultants, and all these issues were also affected by pressure to win matches. The barriers that limit players' creative potential can be attributed to the lack of street soccer (unstructured practice), unadjusted training, the mechanization of play, a decrease in game enjoyment, and narrow game knowledge (Richard et al., 2018; Santos et al., 2016). Furthermore, actual sports systems seem to be unable to overcome these issues, as they have continued to favor a specialized environment, supported in deliberate practice during the early years. Despite the prominence of the deliberate practice approach to expert performance, which encompasses relevant effortful activities done with the specific goal of improving performance, several research studies conducted on the long-term development of creativity devoted attention to deliberate play and unstructured practice during the sampling years (Santos et al., 2020b). The sampling years (ages 6-13) consist of one of the developmental trajectories proposed in the Developmental Model of Sport Participation (DMSP), which focuses on a smooth transition from play to practice (Côté, 1999; Côté & Abernethy, 2012). According to this model, during the sampling years, a diversified practice prevails that encompasses participation in several sports with high levels of deliberate play. Deliberate play is focused on activities that maximize fun and enjoyment and provide immediate gratification (Berry et al., 2008). Players should experience several environments that stimulate physical, technical, tactical, cognitive, affective, and psychosocial aspects, which is considered fertile ground to trigger creative behavior (Santos et al., 2016). Contrary to structured activities, unstructured activities include informal youth-led and spontaneous activities created and adapted to the requirements of the context and environment, like playing street soccer. These types of activities allow players to master important skills by making room for mistakes and providing the chance to discover personally unique ways to use their abilities without pressure from coaches; they also support autonomy and ownership, aiding their development toward P-type creativity (Santos et al., 2016).

Deliberate play should be prioritized during training sessions to generate risk taking and creative moves.

As mentioned previously, players' free play and unstructured leisure activities have been gradually substituted with adult-led formal activities. Clubs should therefore aim to recreate these types of practices that allow youth players to develop and refine their movement patterns while enhancing their adaptability to perform in dynamic environments. In fact, the available literature has reported that these activities contribute to the development of fundamental movement and game skills embodied in a suitable environment for youth players (e.g., it was common to see unbalanced teams during street soccer, where the most competent players faced an inferiority situation—2vs3 or 2vs4—against less skilled children [Pellegrini et al., 2007]). Accordingly, Bowers and colleagues (2014) found a direct positive relation between time spent in unstructured activities during the early years and general creative thinking in the adult years. In this regard, Memmert (2006) found that a six-month deliberate-play intervention program had a beneficial impact on creative tactical performance. Further, Memmert et al. (2010) found that soccer, handball, basketball, and field hockey players—selected by their coaches as being the most creative—spent more time in both structured and unstructured play activities compared to their less-creative counterparts. Likewise, Roca and Ford (2021) demonstrated that highly creative soccer players accumulated more time in free play and unstructured soccer-specific activities, and no differences were identified in soccer-specific formal practice as opposed to less-creative players. Coaches should be aware that an exclusive focus on early specialization can be detrimental for creativity because it stresses a rigid skills-based approach (Richard et al., 2017).

Frameworks and Programs for the Development of Creativity

Driven by the practical goal of building a creativity-supported learning environment, a few proposals for comprehensive frameworks have emerged. During the last few years, to better guide coaches in the development of creativity, several creativity-related frameworks and programs have arisen, such as: (1) the Tactical Creativity Approach (Memmert, 2015a, 2015b); (2) the Creative Developmental Framework (Santos et al., 2016; Santos et al., 2020b), which includes the Skills4Genius program; and (3) the Creative Soccer Platform (Rasmussen & Østergaard, 2016). This last program provides soccer players with opportunities to play and explore different actions that they have never experienced before. By contrast, the Tactical Creativity Approach summarizes Memmert's extensive empirical research, which proposes using the seven D training principles for the training of creativity, which include deliberate practice and play, diversification, deliberate coaching, deliberate memory, deliberate motivation, and one-dimensional games to foster creativity in team sports (Memmert, 2015a, 2015b). Following the previous benchmarks, it is essential to define developmental guidelines from childhood to junior age to nurture an optimal increase in creative behavior. Along this line of reasoning, the Creativity Developmental Framework provides the general approaches that lead to a long-term improvement of creative behavior (Santos et al., 2016). This framework describes five incremental creative stages—(1) the beginner stage (2-6 years), (2) the explorer stage (7-9 years), (3) the illuminati stage (10-12 years), (4) the creator stage (13-15 years), and (5) the rise stage (over 16 years)—and combines them into multidisciplinary approaches infused in creative assumptions. The framework promotes a creativity-friendly environment by combining the following training approaches: diversified practice, physical literacy, nonlinear pedagogy, which encompasses teaching games for understanding (TGfU), a constraint-led approach, and differential learning, and creative thinking (considers divergent and convergent thinking). During the first stages, to ensure a proper creative developmental process, the focus is placed on diversification, deliberate play, and physical literacy grounded by nonlinear pedagogies, which constitute the basis for further development of the players' creative predisposition. Throughout all developmental stages, a nonlinear pedagogy supports in-game centered approaches, which play a key role in triggering more creative tactical-related behaviors. In later stages, progressive sport specialization and the role of variability are extremely important to push the limits of expert players by increasing the range of technical and tactical configurations. Nevertheless, the differential learning embodied in game situations emerges as a promising approach to boost creativity in soccer (Coutinho et al., 2018; Santos et al., 2018).

Be brave enough to suck at something new.

From the previous framework emerged the Skills4Genius, a creativity-based training program that encompasses a set of three constructive models: TGfU, Sport Education, and Student-Designed Games (Santos et al., 2017). After a five-month intervention (for a total of 60 sessions) in elementary school–aged children, the overall findings demonstrated that participants who were engaged in the Skills4Genius program improved their creative thinking and motor performance (Santos et al., 2017). Regarding the in-game creativity components, participants improved creativity as measured by the four aforementioned creativity components in relation to several specific skills (i.e., pass, dribble, shoot) in small-sided game situations (SSG).

Finally, the positional results, collected using GPS devices, demonstrated a higher movement coordination with teammates, suggesting a better knowledge of the principles of the game after the training program. These findings provide an important avenue by which to consider the role of variability in sports training programs. Ultimately, the Skills4Genius findings support an interplay between thinking and sports creativity, revealing commonalities in the underlying processes responsible for driving creative thinking and children's novel behaviors in the field, which is further explored by Richard et al. (2018) and Santos and Monteiro (2020). This program covers a process where children create their own games within certain parameters defined by the teacher or coach (children can co-create). Hence, they have room to explore rules, choose the equipment, methods for scoring, and space (Casey et al., 2011; Hastie & André, 2012). In addition, several active play strategies, such as priming (e.g., playing with superpowers), storytelling (e.g., creating an embodied history during the practice), building material (e.g., creating different balls or goals), and finally, incorporating more and less functional variability by means of differential learning underpinned in SSG situations. According to Ort and colleagues (2017), creative behaviors are promoted by practicing interventions that favor movement variability, which allows players to afford new goal opportunities to trigger a self-organizing process.

CHAPTER 3

The Role of Variability in Performance and Learning

Initially, movement variability was considered to be "noise" resulting from stochastic neuromuscular function, which should be minimized as much as possible to achieve high levels of performance (Shmuelof et al., 2012; Stergiou & Decker, 2011; Stergiou et al., 2013). In fact, it was considered that any movement execution improvement would cause a decrease in the magnitude of movement variability (Barbado Murillo et al., 2017; Caballero et al., 2014; Komar et al., 2015). Inversely, recent reports have suggested that variability may have a functional role in allowing players to have more adaptable movement responses according to the dynamic features of the environment (Chow et al., 2015; Seifert et al., 2013). Accordingly, movement variability seems to reflect the ability of the neuromuscular system to promote diverse motor patterns (Wu et al., 2014) and can be conceived as the multiple variations identified in motor performance that are present across multiple repetitions of a given task (Newell, 1998; Stergiou et al., 2013). Movement variability is inherent to all biological systems, as it is practically impossible to execute the exact same movement in the same precise way, even among expert performers (Stergiou et al., 2013). For example, although the movement of Cristiano Ronaldo looks similar when striking the ball during a free kick, the distance between the feet, the distance to the ball, the angle to the target, the speed of movement when moving toward the ball, and the zone where his foot contacts the ball always change slightly. Also, if we account for the way motor units are recruited or even the weather conditions, we may assume that it is impossible to reproduce any movement in the exact same fashion (Bernshtein, 1967). From this viewpoint, it is important not to misconceive this variability with the variability found in beginners that reveals a lack of movement control (Seifert et al., 2013). Movement variability should be considered as adaptive and flexible movement patterns (Pesce et al., 2019).

Currently, there has been an increase in the amount of available research emphasizing the key role of variability in promoting learning (Herzfeld & Shadmehr, 2014; Tumer & Brainard, 2007; Wu et al., 2014), movement adaptability (Seifert et al., 2013), and fostering creative predisposition (Santos et al., 2016; Santos et al., 2017; Santos et al., 2020a). These benefits have led to a renewed interest in understanding the effects of increasing the level of variability to improve performance, mainly in team sport settings. The environment has a major role in the players' decisions, as it contains informational properties that the players use to support their decisions (Seifert et al., 2013; Travassos et al., 2012a). Under this scope, the variability can be functional when it relates to the players' ability to adjust their movements as a result of changes in dynamic performance contexts (Caso & van der Kamp, 2020; Davids et al., 2003; Farrow & Robertson, 2017; Glazier & Davids, 2009). An example is when a goalkeeper has to strike the ball during a goal kick under different weather conditions. Striking the ball when the weather is windy may require the goalkeeper to strike in a different direction, using the wind to direct the ball toward the intention zone. This movement pattern would be different if it were performed on a sunny day with no wind. Similarly, the way the foot contacts the ball and the force applied to pass the ball to a teammate (e.g., central defender) would differ depending on the extent of the opposing team's pressure.

These examples highlight how variable movement patterns emerge during competitive scenarios. Accordingly, training with additional variability seems to support players in acquiring functional movement patterns to act within dynamic competitive environments (Chow et al., 2015). That is, exposing players to a broad range of variable practice scenarios will enhance their movement adaptability (Santos et al., 2018). From this perspective, movement variability can be enhanced by the dynamic change in the task rules or movement boundaries during the practice (Caballero et al., 2014; Hristovski et al., 2011; Orth et al., 2017; Schöllhorn et al., 2006; Stergiou et al., 2006). Taking this into consideration, the following sections show how to increase the level of variability by manipulating individual and task-related boundaries and present research surrounding the acute and chronic effects of training with variability.

Differential Learning

Over the last few decades, a theoretical approach has emerged called Differential Learning, which embraces the inclusion of variability as a way to promote learning and improve performance (Frank et al., 2008; Schöllhorn et al., 2006;

Schöllhorn et al., 2009). Accordingly, this approach explores fluctuations in the movement system by including continuous perturbations with no movement repetition and without verbal feedback, which then challenges the players to deal with the disturbances in the competitive environment (Schöllhorn et al., 2009; Schollhorn et al., 2012). By increasing the level of movement fluctuations, the system faces instabilities while searching for the stable state of an optimal mode (Schöllhorn & Horst, 2019). That is, this additional variability will guide the learner to explore and discover individualized movement solutions, as the solution that works for one player may not work for others (Schollhorn et al., 2009). This process enhances the players' movement adaptability, leading to novel and functional movement patterns. More specifically, this approach consists of adding infinite movement variations with the aim of continuously challenging the players to explore and adapt their movement patterns (Schollhorn et al., 2006; Schöllhorn et al., 2009). To do so, several manipulations in the boundary conditions are performed, such as varying the ball type, size, weight, shape, and number of balls; playing with different body restrictions (e.g., with the right arm in abduction, with both hands on the chest, or with arms crossed); playing with the manipulation of the equipment (e.g., playing with an eye patch or playing while holding a ball with two hands); playing on pitches of different shapes (e.g., square, circle, triangle, diamond, or hexagon), surfaces (e.g., grass, dirt, sand, or cement), or angles (e.g., declined pitches or irregular surfaces); adding obstacles (e.g., tchoukball, wooden benches, or inflatable men or tape to obstruct the path); or manipulating the rules (e.g., playing hand by hand with a teammate or with an opponent or playing with the hands and feet).

These manipulations are intended to expose the players to a broad range of variable conditions that allow them to better reorganize their skills and develop new and functional movement patterns (Santos et al., 2016; Schöllhorn et al., 2006). For example, developing the kicking action under different variations may improve the player's adaptability to kick when confronting unstable situations (e.g., when opponents are pressing), allowing them to better adjust their movement behavior.

This approach has also been associated with higher brain activation (increased alpha and theta waves) compared to more traditional and prescriptive approaches (Henz & Schöllhorn, 2016), which has been linked to higher rates of learning. Accordingly, it seems that exposing players to a wide range of movement variations contributes to an overload of the prefrontal cortex information due to the considerable number of decisions related to the action to be performed, thus enhancing the working memory of the motor control system (Schöllhorn et al., 2009; Schöllhorn et al., 2012).

Hence, Farrow and Robertson (2017) proposed a skill acquisition periodization framework, which suggests different approaches that promote a continuum of variability (from constant to differential practices).

According to the findings of previous studies, differential learning practice promotes superior skills in both the acquisition and retention phase (Farrow & Robertson, 2017; Hossner et al., 2016; Pabel et al., 2018; Schöllhorn et al., 2009). These insights have aroused researchers' interest in exploring the effects of differential learning on players' behavior. Overall, the findings show better results in interventions sustained by differential learning over more repetitive approaches (Coutinho et al., 2018; Gaspar et al., 2019; Santos et al., 2018; Schöllhorn et al., 2009; Schöllhorn et al., 2012).

"It's not about the number of hours you practice, it's about the number of hours your mind is present during the practice."

–Kobe Bryant

Evidence-Based Interventions

Previous sections have approached the essential concepts and benefits of increasing the level of variability during practice tasks. As mentioned earlier, these benefits have drawn interest in research related to the use of variability to improve performance, prompting two main lines of research: (1) acute effects of variability, in which players are usually exposed to a condition with less variability and then to a condition with significant variability (at which point, their performance is compared between conditions); and (2) chronic effects of variability, by implementing training interventions that are usually compared with more traditional training approaches. The following chapter presents prior research related to both approaches and the main findings.

Short-Term Effects of Variability

Although most of the research on variability has focused on exploring mid- to long-term changes as a result of training interventions, more recently, a few studies have explored how acutely additional variability affects players' performance during more analytical and game-based situations (see figures 2 and 3). For instance, one study explored how youth soccer players' (under 15 years of age) kicking and jumping performance varied as a result of performing a training session sustained by variability compared to a more traditional training session (Gaspar et al., 2019). The training session consisted of kicking 36 balls toward the goal from three different locations marked along the penalty area using two different approaches: (1) 18 static balls (6 per position) and (2) 18 balls kicked after a 5-meter run (6 per position). What varied between the interventions was the way the players struck the ball. In the traditional session, the players were encouraged to kick with maximum accuracy and speed toward the goal in a standardized way; however, each repetition performed in the session with additional variability consisted of kicking in unconventional ways, such as kicking while wearing an eye patch, with both arms crossed, while clapping in front and behind, or even while hopping on one leg (Gaspar et al., 2019). Players' kicking was evaluated based on their speed and accuracy toward the goal with different point zones, and their vertical jump ability was measured using the countermovement jump protocol over three different periods: (1) a baseline test, performed on a different day; (2) a post-test measurement performed immediately after finishing the traditional/variability session; and (3) a re-assessment following a simulated 35-minute 11vs11 football match. Compared to the traditional intervention, overall, the differential intervention improved the speed of the kick and countermovement jump from the baseline to the post-test; it also improved the player's accuracy toward more complex zones from the baseline to the post-match assessment (Gaspar et al., 2019).

Despite the low magnitude, the results suggested that the intervention supported by variability was beneficial for improving not only the kicking accuracy and speed but also the vertical jump performance, and even from an acute effect, it was possible to identify small improvements in players' performance. However, as this study consisted of a more analytical task, it was equally important to inspect how acutely the players' performance could be affected during a game situation.

Therefore, one study explored how different pitch configurations affected the physical and positional performance during small-sided games with youth players from two developmental age groups (under-13 and under-15) (Coutinho et al., 2019). The conditions explored in the study were (a) a regular pitch, designed like that of a regular competitive game; (b) a sided pitch (higher width than length), meaning a pitch with a greater width than length; (c) a different orientation pitch, designed with a different orientation to those used for an official match; the pitch was similar in size to the regular pitch, but it was designed from lateral to lateral line in contrast to end line; and (d) a dynamic pitch, in which the players performed on three different pitches, including a regular pitch, a narrow pitch, and a diamond-shaped pitch. This last condition was considered to have additional variability, as the players had to dynamically adjust their behavior every minute (for 6 mins) and adjust to the pitch boundaries. In most cases, the results demonstrated low values of movement synchronization—consisting of a variable intended to measure the amount of time that players moved in the same direction (higher values usually mean better performances [Folgado et al., 2017])—and lower values of distance covered at different speed intensities during the dynamic condition compared to the regular condition (Coutinho et al., 2019).

Using a similar approach, a more recent study explored how youth players' performance was affected by playing with different types of balls: (a) play with a football for 6 mins; (b) play with a rugby ball for 6 mins; (c) play with a handball for 6 mins; and (d) play in a mixed condition, where the ball was changed every two minutes of the game among those listed above (for 6 mins) (Santos et al., 2020a). In addition, the authors tested these scenarios with two small-sided games: Gk+4vs4+Gk (4-a-side) and Gk+6vs6+Gk (6-a-side). The comparison with the ball in the mixed condition (additional variability) revealed decreases in passing and dribbling performance (mostly in 6-a-side), lower physical demands (especially in 6-a-side), and lower team dispersion (especially in 4-a-side). The findings from both studies suggest that players may encounter more difficulties sustaining their behavior based on the information available in the environment when facing scenarios with additional variability (Santos et al., 2020a).

These results contrast with those identified in the first study presented in this section. However, even though the players completed a session with additional variability during the first study, their performance was measured without variability, so it may be possible that the players' performance might also be different if the dynamic condition were used to promote variability, but the players' performance is then assessed using a regular condition.

From a general perspective, the first study showed that acute kicking performance may be enhanced following training tasks surrounded by additional variability, while the second and third studies highlighted that players may experience more difficulties identifying and using the relevant information from the environment when exposed to additional variability.

More recently, two new studies explored how players' performances were affected by acute manipulations in the task boundary conditions. For instance, Coutinho et al. (2022) exposed the players to four conditions during a Gk+6vs6+Gk: 1) control condition, where the players were only instructed to play in the 1-2-3-1 playing system; 2) individual condition, where apart from using the previous system, players were instructed to play with body restrictions varied at every minute (i.e., from 0 to 1 min, play with arms crossed; from 1 to 2 min, play with the hands on the back; from 2 to 3 min, play with arms down, holding the shorts; from 3 to 4 min, play with arms elevated; from 4 to 5 min, play with left hand touching the head; and from 5 to 6 min, play with right hand touching the head); 3) collective variability, players were instructed to vary the playing system at every minute (i.e., from 0 to 1 min, 1-2-3-1; from 1 to 2 min, 1-3-2-1; from 2 to 3 min, 1-2-2-2; from 3 to 4 min, 1-1-3-2; from 4 to 5 min, 1-1-4-1; and from 5 to 6 min, 1-3-1-2); and 4) mixed condition, in which the conditions from both the individual and collective were applied together (e.g., from 2 to the 3 min, players performed in the 1-2-2-2 system while also having the arms down holding the shorts). Each condition seemed to affect the players differently, according to the type of boundary conditions applied. For instance, applying individual restrictions mostly affected the players' positional performances, as the players may have focused on individual technique to face the demands imposed by the body restrictions. In turn, constantly asking the players to explore different playing systems (i.e., collective condition) led the players to explore more space and, consequently, increase the physical demands (Coutinho et al., 2022).

Surprisingly, the mixed condition revealed similar values in all variables to those found in the CTR, which may suggest that players adopt more stable behaviors when facing conditions with high levels of variability. In addition, Santos et al. (forthcoming) explored how varying the number of opposing creative opponents affects youth players' creative, technical, and tactical responses during SSG. A total of 60 soccer players from three age groups: (U9, U11, and U13) were tested during a 4-a-side plus goalkeeper SSG to be ranked according to their creative potential. Based on this rank, four players with medium creative potential were assigned to an intermediate team for each age group that was kept constant across all data collection. This intermediate team faced a competition scenario against an opponent team with one, two, three, and four players ranked with high creative potential (1C, 2C, 3C, and 4C, respectively). Findings revealed that moderate and high demanding scenarios prompted the emergence of new behaviors (i.e., from 1C

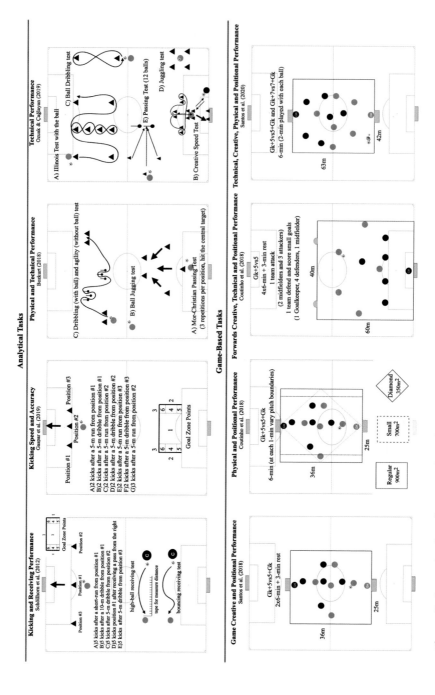

Figure 2. Example of testing procedures in research focused on variability.

Short-Term Interventions (Acute Effects)

	Kicking Speed and Accuracy Gaspar et al. (2019)	Physical and Positional Performance Coutinho et al. (2018)	Technical, Creative, Physical and Positional Performance Santos et al. (2020)	Technical, Physical and Positional Performance Coutinho et al. (2022)	Technical, Creative and Positional Performance Santos et al. (2022, forthcoming)
Technical	↓ Kicking accuracy (1 and 5 points zone) ↑ Kicking accuracy (4 and 6 points zone) ↑ Kicking speed (km/h)		↓ Successful Passes (n° of actions; 4-a-side, 6-a-side) ↓ Successful Dribbles (n° of actions; 6-a-side)		
Creative			↓ Fluency (n° of actions; 6-a-side)		↓ Creative Score (U9 vs + Creatives)
Physical	↑ Jumping performance (cmj, countermovement jump)	↑ Total distance covered (m) ↓ Dist. covered at low intensities (0.0 - 6.9 km/h) ↑ Dist. covered at moderate intensities (7.0 - 15.9 km/h) ↓ Dist. covered at high intensities (≥ 16.0 km/h)	↑ Total distance covered (m; 4-a-side, 6-a-side) ↓ Jogging distance (3.6 - 14.3 km/h; 4-a-side, 6-a-side) ↓ Running distance (14.4 - 19.8 km/h; 6-a-side) ↓ Sprinting distance (≥19.9 km/h; 6-a-side) ↑ Dist. covered while walking (0.0 - 3.5 km/h; 4/6-a-side)	↑ Running Distance (m; Col > Ctr / Ind. / Mix.) ↑ Sprinting Distance (m; Col. > Ctr. / Ind. / Mix.)	
Positional		↑ Effective Playing Space (m²; U13, U15) ↓ Longitudinal Synchronization (%; U13, U15) ↓ Lateral Synchronization (%; U13, U15)	↓ Spatial exploration index (m; 4-a-side) ↓ Distance between teammates (m; 4-a-side) ↓ Distance between teams centroids (m; 4-a-side)	↓ Dist. Nearest Opp. (m; Ind > Mix.) ↑ Spatial exploration index (m; Col > Ctr.) ↑ Long. Synchronization (%; Mix. > Col / Ind.) ↑ Lat. Synchronization (%; Ctr > Ind. / Col. / Mix.)	Spatial explor. index (m; ↑U9, ↓U11 / U13 vs + Creatives) ↑ Dist. to team / opp. centroid (%CV; U9 vs + Creatives) ↓ Dist. to team / opp. centroid (Agifte; U11 vs + Creatives) ↑ Dist. to team / opp. centroid (Agifte; U13 vs + Creatives)

Figure 3. Main study's findings regarding movement variability in relation to short-term interventions.

41

to 3C), while extremely high demanding scenarios (i.e., 4C) seemed to inhibit all the creativity components. Overall, adding creative players mostly impacted the team's collective behavior rather than creativity components and technical-related skills.

Outstanding players have a new to challenge themselves every moment and possess an innovative attitude.

Coaches might grasp how players from different age groups adjust their behavior according to the profile of the opposing team. Indeed, a main challenge for coaches is to uncover the role of boundary conditions in releasing creative behaviors according to the players' levels. In this regard, it seems vital to expose players to varied and dynamic contexts that challenge them to think and behave beyond the typical.

Mid- and Long-Term Effects of Variability

Research interest in variability is somewhat recent; nevertheless, some studies have already started to explore how mid- to long-term training interventions sustained by variability affect players' performance in both analytical and game-based tasks (see figure 4).

One study explored how adult-level players' (about 24 years old) kicking and ball receiving performance was modified after a four-week training intervention (twice a week) based on two approaches: (1) a traditional intervention and (2) an intervention sustained by variability (blocked and random) (Schöllhorn et al., 2012). Players underwent pre-, post-, and retention testing focused on the ability to receive two balls (a high ball with the chest and a second high ball that bounced on the ground prior to the reception) with the minimum space possible and to kick with precision to a target. In both groups, 20 exercises for ball reception and kicking were performed for 25 minutes per session. The tasks performed by the traditional group involved repeating similar types of movement with a focus on the technique requirements and with corrective verbal feedback. By contrast, the groups that trained with variability were required to practice the same number of actions but add a different type of fluctuation to each repetition to promote variability (e.g., first ball reception, receive the ball with one eye closed and each arm in a different position; second ball reception, stand on one foot and rotate both arms forward) (Schöllhorn et al., 2012). Overall, higher values were identified in the groups that trained with variability for both movement techniques and across all measurements compared to the traditional intervention, suggesting its superiority over more traditional approaches.

Similar findings have been found by more recent literature using a four-week intervention (three sessions per week, 20 minutes per session) and an eight-week intervention (three sessions per week, 40 to 50 minutes each session); two groups (experimental [variability] and control [traditional]) were also exposed to technical-based interventions over that period (Bozkurt, 2018; Ozuak & Çaglayan, 2019). Players' performance was evaluated using standardized passing, dribbling, juggling, and agility tests. Although only significant differences were discovered for the dribbling and agility tests, with higher values being present for the variability group, the players who enrolled in the variability program improved more than the traditional group for all tests (Bozkurt, 2018; Ozuak & Çaglayan, 2019).

Using more ecological settings, two studies explored how players' performance modified over a 10-week period (two sessions per week) (Coutinho et al., 2018) and over a five-month period (three sessions per week) (Santos et al., 2018) as a result of enrolling in training interventions involving variability. The first study recruited youth forward players from two different age groups (under 15 years of age and under 17 years of age) to expose them to a training intervention of physical literacy and small-sided games performed with additional variability. Accordingly, the forwards that trained with variability performed approximately 10 minutes of physical literacy exercises with additional variability (e.g., doing ladder drills while rotating a ball around the hips), followed by 1vs1+Gk situation in a triangular pitch and using a small ball, followed by 15 minutes of small-sided games with variability (e.g., at each 30 seconds, vary the number of players involved—5vs5, 3vs4, 2vs2, 1vs3—or play with different pitch shapes), while the forwards in the control group performed regular training sessions with the remaining group (Coutinho et al., 2018). After the intervention, the players who enrolled in the intervention sustained by variability improved their ability to dribble (under 15), shoot (under 15 and under), and score goals (under 15), developed their fluency and versatility components of creativity (under 15), and revealed a higher movement unpredictability (under 17) compared to the control group (Coutinho et al., 2018). Although the results were more evident in the younger age group, significant improvements in players' behaviors were identified in both ages, suggesting that training with variability is beneficial to specific playing position behaviors.

Long-Term Interventions (Chronic Effects)

	Kicking and Receiving Performance — Schöllhorn et al. (2012)	Physical and Technical Performance — Bozkurt (2018)	Technical Performance — Ozuak & Çağlayan (2019)	Game Creative and Positional Performance — Santos et al. (2018)	Forwards Creative, Technical and Positional Performance — Coutinho et al. (2018)
Technical	↑ Kicking accuracy (total points) ↑ Receiving accuracy (distance)	= Juggling (higher values for DL) = Passing (higher values for DL) ⇐ Dribbling (higher values for DL)	↑ Dribbling course		↑ Successful dribbles (n° of actions; U15) ↑ Successful shots (n° of actions; U15, U17) ↑ Goals (n° of actions; U15)
Creative				↓ Fails (n° of actions; U13, U15) ↑ Attempts (n° of actions; U13) ↑ Versatility (n° of actions; U13, U15) ↑ Originality (n° of actions; U13, U15)	↑ Fluency (n° of actions; U15) ↑ Attempts (n° of actions; U15) ↑ Versatility (n° of actions; U15)
Physical		↑ Agility	↑ Agility		↑ Jumping performance (countermovement jump; U15, U17) ↑ Repeated change of direction (seconds; U15)
Positional				↑ Distance to teammates regularity (ApEn; U13, U15) ↑ Distance to target regularity (ApEn; U13, U15)	↑ Spatial exploration index (indiv. area explored - m; U17) ↑ Stretch index (dispersion measure; U15) ↑ Longitudinal movement irregularity (ApEn; U17) ↑ Lateral movement irregularity (ApEn; U17)

Figure 4. Main study findings regarding movement variability in relation to long-term interventions.

In the second study, the authors explored the effects of performing small-sided games with additional variability (e.g., playing with different balls, on different surfaces, and with different types of body movements) in relation to regular small-sided games (e.g., using neutral players and limiting touches) in two developmental age groups (under 13 and under 15) (Santos et al., 2018). After the training intervention, the players revealed improvements in the creative predisposition, mainly in the originality, versatility, and attempt components of creativity, and they promoted more regular movement behaviors, suggesting higher game awareness compared to the group that performed traditional small-sided games (Santos et al., 2018).

In summary, the results from these studies showed improvements in specific technical actions (receiving and kicking) and in-game performance as a result of exposing players to training practices surrounded by variability. In addition, this variability seems to trigger players' creative predisposition and promotes more adaptable technical patterns, possibly by exposing them to a broad range of movement solutions and a higher game awareness that may result from continuously acting on dynamic environments that require players to be attuned to relevant information (Coutinho et al., 2018; Santos et al., 2018). Despite the available literature, there is little guidance on the appropriate degree of variability for specific levels of performers. In this vein, chapter 5 will provide some insights on how to periodize within the soccer context.

PART II

Designing Training Tasks

CHAPTER 4

Adding Variability

Part I of this book highlighted the theoretical and scientific background related to the use of variability in training practices. This second part mainly provides examples of training tasks with additional variability. To assist coaches in understanding the tasks and provide a general picture that variability can be added to any type of training task aim (e.g., psychological, physical, technical, and tactical), four different categories of exercises were created (see figure 5). The first category, nano-level tasks, are mostly analytical drills that intend to increase the players' movement repertoire (e.g., striking 12 balls with different movement patterns, such as with hands tied, one arm raised up, and while being pushed). The second category, micro-level tasks, consists of 1vs1 situations, where players experience, during more game-based contexts, the skills developed at the nano-level (e.g., 1vs1 with an eye patch on a pitch full of obstacles, such as training mannequins, wooden benches, and pitch markers). The third category

Nano-Level (Motor Exploration) Tasks	Corresponds to tasks intended to promote motor exploration and increase the players' movement repertoire.
Micro-Level Tasks	Consists of opposition-based scenarios (e.g., 1vs1) in which players use the skills learned during the nano level to overcome opponents.
Meso-Level Tasks	Based on cooperative interactions under variable and dynamic conditions using mostly small-sided games as the context. Focused on the development of principles of play at the group level.
Macro-Level Game-Based Tasks	Players are exposed to large game scenarios (e.g., 7vs7) that include dynamic variations of the rules to promote movement adaptability. For example, players could play on a pitch where the boundary shapes vary (e.g., diamond, triangle, circular, etc.), or the team's tactical formation varies each minute of the game.

Figure 5. Categorization of the training tasks.

consists of meso-level tasks, which explore the players' cooperative and competitive tendencies (e.g., 3vs3 playing under a pitch with different surfaces while implementing different types of balls). The fourth category relates to macro-level tasks, which include a more pronounced tactical focus in larger game situations (e.g., varying the pitch shape and size in a dynamical perspective [i.e., every minute, so that the offensive and defensive players have to adapt their behaviors to the available space]).

Nano-Level Tasks

The Creator

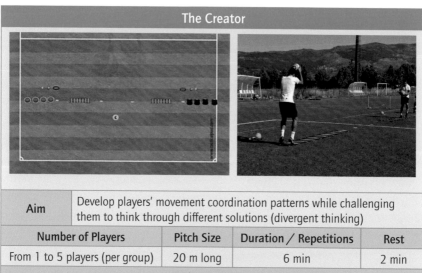

Aim	Develop players' movement coordination patterns while challenging them to think through different solutions (divergent thinking)		
Number of Players	**Pitch Size**	**Duration / Repetitions**	**Rest**
From 1 to 5 players (per group)	20 m long	6 min	2 min

Task Description

This task focuses on challenging players' ability to create new ways to move. For that purpose, each player will have to perform one movement on the agility ladder, return back, and then touch the next teammate's hand. The second player will then have to move down the ladder in a different way (e.g., if teammate performed in and out while moving the arms up and down, the second and subsequent players must explore other movement types). To guarantee motivation and focus, both teams will compete against each other, and the team that performs more different movements will be the winner. Accordingly, the red player starts to do one movement, and while returning back, a blue player (belonging to the opposing team) will perform a different movement in relation to the red player. The task ends when one of the teams is not able to perform any different movements.

Adding Variability

Add material to the task (e.g., different types of balls, agility poles, ropes) to allow players to integrate these features into their movements. Also, coaches may ask the players to move in groups of two (e.g., while holding agility poles).

Task Material

2 agility ladders; 6 agility poles (of 3 different colors); 8 soccer balls

The Race

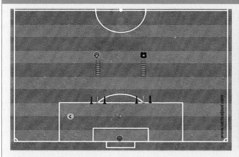 

Aim	Develop players' movement coordination patterns and 1vs1 skills		
Number of Players	**Pitch Size**	**Duration / Repetitions**	**Rest**
From 2 to 10 players	30 m from the target	2 sets / 4 reps	30 sec per rep 90 sec per set

Task Description

The task occurs in a Gk+1vs1 situation. Before each repetition, the coach will define the movement to be performed on the ladder (e.g., side shuffle). In addition to the movement defined, the athlete carries a soccer ball in the dominant hand that he uses to move around the trunk (foot–hand coordination). After the stimulus (coach's whistle, light, or other type of visual or sound stimulus), both players start to perform the pre-defined movement in the agility ladder (varied at every repetition). Before the players finish the pre-defined movements on the agility ladder, the coach will specify the color of the agility pole that the players must go around before moving to the 1vs1. Following, the coach will throw a soccer ball using the rebounder (tchoukball), and the first player to reach the ball will have the opportunity to score while the other players try to prevent them from scoring. This task can be performed in a competition basis (1vs1 or in several groups).

Adding Variability

Modify the players' movement with the soccer ball during the agility ladder portion of the drill (e.g., soccer ball rotation around the trunk), score using different ball types, or include body constraints when shooting (e.g., both hands on the air or both hands on the chest).

Task Material

2 agility ladders; 6 agility poles (of 3 different colors); 8 soccer balls; different types of ball

Like M. Jordan

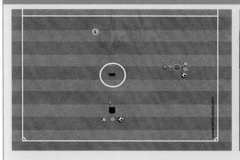 

Aim	Develop players' ability to create new movement patterns and think through different movement solutions (divergent thinking)		
Number of Players	**Pitch Size**	**Duration / Repetitions**	**Rest**
From 1 to 5 players (per team)	10×10 m	6 min	2 min

Task Description

This task focuses on increasing players' abilities to create new forms of movement. With this in mind, the player tries to put the soccer ball inside the box using a different way or movement each time. To increase the players' motivation and focus, the task can be competitive (e.g., the first player will try to put the soccer ball in the box in a specific way, then the second player will try to put the soccer ball in the box but in a way that differs from the first player, and so on). The task ends when a player is unable to perform a different movement or time runs out. One point is awarded for each different movement, and two points are awarded when the ball is put inside the box.

Adding Variability

Add material to the task (e.g., different types of balls, agility poles, ropes) and ask players to integrate them with the movement.

Task Material

1 box; 5 soccer balls; different types of balls

Hitman

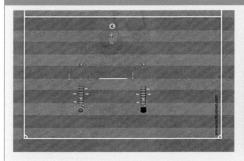

Aim	Develop coordinative movement patterns and shooting skills under variable scenarios		
Number of Players	Pitch Size	Duration / Repetitions	Rest
From 2 to 10 players	30×20 m	2 sets / 5 reps (1 rep = ladder, turning around the cone and kicking the ball to the target)	30 sec per rep 90 sec per set

Task Description

The task is performed individually in a relay race format. Following the signal (sound or visual) to start, both players begin the agility ladder by placing their foot according to the flat markers (left side = left foot; right side = right foot; two sides = both feet; only inside = choose foot). While doing this, the players should do opposite ball movements (e.g., left foot outside, rotate trunk with soccer ball to the right; one step inside = extend arms with the ball). Following another signal (e.g., yellow / green color, or the coach moving left or right to simulate defender), players move backwards to the corresponding cone (e.g., coach moving to the right cone would mean that the player moves to the left cone). After turning around the cone, they accelerate to the white line, trying to hit the person with the ball.

Adding Variability

Modify the ball type (e.g., rugby, reflex ball), include body constraints (e.g., arms in abduction), or use obstacles (e.g., agility poles, ropes linked with agility poles for players to jump or duck under) before the white line.

Task Material

10 flat markers, 2 cones; 4 agility poles (of 2 different colors), 10 soccer balls; 1 training mannequin

Be the Fastest

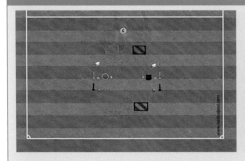 

Aim	Develop reaction and acceleration speed coupled with the ability to travel with different types of balls		
Number of Players	**Pitch Size**	**Duration / Repetitions**	**Rest**
From 2 to 10 players	30×20 m	3 sets/4 reps (1 rep = turning the agility pole and traveling with the ball to the square)	30 sec per rep 90 sec per set

Task Description

The task is performed individually in a relay race format. To start, the coach will say a number (even or uneven), which will inform the players to where they have to travel (even to the right, uneven to the left), followed by a color (red, green, yellow), which will inform the players which soccer ball to travel to. When the task begins, the players will turn around agility pole, find the ball to which they've been assigned, and travel with it to the square.

Adding Variability

Combine the movement of travel with the ball with body restrictions (e.g., hands on the back of the head). Include obstacles in the space so that the players must turn around (e.g., training mannequins). Change the square by adding goals, and the first to score wins (see right-hand side figure).

Task Material

8 flat markers; 2 cones; 6 agility poles (3 different colors, 2 of each color); 6 balls (3 different types, 2 of each type)

Move Like an Animal

Aim	Develop movement coordination patterns coupled with the ability to travel with different types of balls		
Number of Players	**Pitch Size**	**Duration / Repetitions**	**Rest**
From 2 to 10 players	30×20 m	3 sets/4 reps (1 rep = moving over the hurdles, picking the ball, and traveling with it)	30 sec per rep 90 sec per set

Task Description

The task is performed individually in a relay race format. To start, players will pick a card with a specific animal on it (e.g., frog, monkey, cat, fish). Next, the players will alternate going underneath and over the barriers, using movements that mimic those used by the animal featured on their chosen card (e.g., if their card shows a frog, the player will perform the course as a frog). To finish, players will pick the colored ball specified by the coach and travel with it to the opponent's marker, using the same animal movements as before. The first to pick the ball and travel with it to the opponent's marker wins.

Adding Variability

Change animal movements at each repetition. Include storytelling, where the coach or other players tell a story involving animals (e.g., "now the frog faces a cliff and has to jump") and the players have to perform the story.

Task Material

14 flat markers; 4 hurdles (~40 cm); 2 hurdles (~15-20 cm); 6 soccer balls (3 different colors, 2 of each color)

The Equilibrist

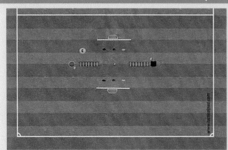 

Aim	Develop coordinative movement patterns and 1vs1 dribbling skills		
Number of Players	Pitch Size	Duration / Repetitions	Rest
From 2 to 10 players	~30 m long and 20 m wide	4 sets/2 reps (1 rep = stepping on both colors, picking the ball, and attempting to score/stay on the ball)	30 sec/rep 90 sec/set

Task Description

At the signal (either visual or sound), both players start to perform a pre-defined movement in the agility ladder (i.e., to be defined by the coach at each repetition) while throwing a tennis ball into the air with one hand. Before ending the movement on the agility ladder, the coach will specify the marker color that the players will have to step on (e.g., if the coach says blue, each player must step on the blue marker closest to them and then step on the blue marker from the opposite row) before they can try to score. The first player that reaches the soccer ball (i.e., after stepping on both blue markers) can pick the ball from the middle and attempt to score in one of the two targets (defined by the agility poles).

Adding Variability

Vary at every repetition the movement on the agility ladder. Include two tennis ball to be thrown into the air during the agility ladder (instead of only one). Go to both sides (instead of only one). Attribute numbers to colors and add math calculations (e.g., blue from 1 to 10, red from 11 to 19, and yellow from 20 to 30; if the coach says, "five times five," players would step to yellow). Change scoring mode (e.g., cross the line with the ball or just keep possession for five seconds by protecting the ball).

Task Material

2 agility ladders; 6 agility poles (of 3 different colors); 8 soccer balls

The Astronaut

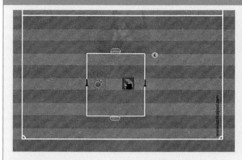 

Aim	Develop spatial perception and ball receiving skills		
Number of Players	**Pitch Size**	**Duration / Repetitions**	**Rest**
From 2 to 10 players	~30 m long and 20 m wide	4 sets / 4 reps (1 rep = 1 pass to a teammate)	30 sec / rep 90 sec / set

Task Description

Each player begins by holding a soccer ball. The task consists of a 1vs1 situation. At the signal (either visual or sound), the player will pass the ball through the air to their teammate. The ball must hit the teammate's square. If the ball falls out of the square, the player who passed the ball would be considered the loser; if the teammate fails to receive the ball, that player would be considered the loser.

Adding Variability

Pass in different ways (e.g., using the ankle). When a player catches the teammate's soccer ball, have him place it on the ground and perform 1vs1 at one or both targets. Instead of passing to a teammate, require players to throw the ball into the air to the opposing box and catch it in that box (see right-hand side figure). Ask both players to pass the balls along the ground to the opponent (both players pass their balls to the teammate at the same time according to the specified signal), then leave the ball on the square, and, depending on the number called by the coach (e.g., 1 – the player should turn around the closest agility pole, 2 – the farther one), accelerate to the corresponding agility pole. When returning to the square, the player kicks the ball into the target. Vary the type of balls used.

Task Material

8 flat markers; 2 agility poles; 2 small goals; 2 soccer balls

The Sprinter

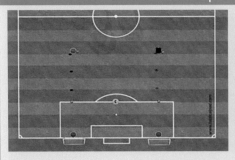 

Aim	Develop sprinting and finishing skills with body restrictions		
Number of Players	**Pitch Size**	**Duration / Repetitions**	**Rest**
From 1 to 12 players	40 m from the target	2 sets / 3 reps (1 rep = moving between each marker and shooting into the target)	30 sec / rep 90 sec / set

Task Description

The task is performed individually in a relay race format. Players hold a soccer ball in their hands. Between each marker, they have to change the movement with the ball (e.g., first, arms flexed 90 degrees while holding the ball; second, arms flexed 180 degrees while holding the ball above the head) and then try to score a goal. The first to shoot wins two points, and the first to score a goal wins three points. This reinforces players' trunk stability while also developing their power ability. The ball can be substituted with a disk (e.g., approximately 5 kgs).

Adding Variability

Use an agility pole instead of a ball (see right-hand side figure). Kick different types of balls. Instead of being performed by only one player, combine the task with groups of two players who will sprint together while holding the agility pole.

Task Material

6 flat markers; 2 regular goals; 4 soccer balls; different types of balls

The Sniper

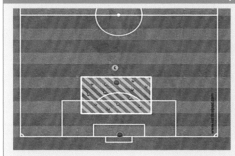 

Aim	Develop finishing skills with additional muscular fatigue

Number of Players	Pitch Size	Duration / Repetitions	Rest
From 2 to 10 players	15×20 m	~2 min (per player)	2 min

Task Description

Each player will have 15 balls in a specific space. The goal is for the player to kick all the balls into the target in as many different ways as possible. The player will have two minutes to kick all the balls, and one point will be awarded if a goal is scored plus three points for each different way they perform the kick. To increase motivation and focus, players or teams can compete.. For example, four players start inside, and each has one goal defended by a goalkeeper. At the signal (either visual or sound), they will have to pick a ball and shoot to the corresponding target. The number of goals shot by each player will be dependent on their ability to perform the task quickly.

Adding Variability

Kick different types of balls (see right-hand side figure), use different movement patterns (e.g., at every kick one different body restriction movement such as hands in the air or hands crossed), or vary the type of target (e.g., small goals, boxes, basketball).

Task Material

4 markers; 15 different types of balls; 1 regular goal

Manyballs

Aim	
Develop reaction skills and the ability to score under different conditions	
Number of Players	**Pitch Size**
From 2 to 10 players	20 m long
Duration / Repetitions	**Rest**
4 sets/2 reps (1 rep = picking a ball, traveling with, it and shooting to the target)	30 sec/rep 90 sec/set

Task Description

The task is performed individually in a relay race format. At the signal (either visual or sound), players should accelerate to the first soccer ball defined by the coach and then dribble it while juggling the other ball like they would a basketball (i.e., one ball is being moved with the foot while the other is being dribbled with the hand). When they arrive at the box, they should try to score. After, the players will accelerate to the second ball defined by the coach and repeat the same action until all balls have been shot. The player with the most goals scored within the defined time would be considered the winner.

Adding Variability

Vary the method of scoring (e.g., put the soccer ball inside of a box). Add obstacles to force the players to find different ways of scoring. Rather than score in the small goal, the task can be performed into a regular target defended by a goalkeeper, where the players would have to put the ball in the zone (blue/red) and then accelerate into the penalty box to take the soccer ball; the first player to do so will kick.

Task Material

2 flat markers; 2 small goals; 2 soccer ball; 8 balls (4 different types, 2 of each)

58

Mountain Climber

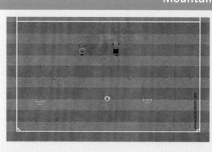

Aim	
Develop players' sprinting ability under inclined planes coupled with finishing skills	
Number of Players	**Pitch Size**
From 2 to 12	15 m long
Duration / Repetitions	**Rest**
3 sets/2 reps (1 rep = sprinting with the weight, picking the ball, and shooting at the target)	45 sec/ rep 2 min/set

Task Description

The task is performed individually in a relay race format. After the signal (either visual or sound), both players travel the distance from the starting position to the end position (ball zone) with their arms extended while holding a 5 kg weight. When approaching the ball zone, keeping hold of the weight, they should attempt to shoot the ball and score on the target. The first player to shoot the ball and score wins.

Adding Variability

Use different types of balls. Include body movements with the weight while sprinting (e.g., continuously flexing and extending the arms with the weight). While being an individual task, it can also be performed in a relay race mode, where each player will cover a specific space with the weight, pass it to a teammate, and so on until the last teammate arrives at the last station, where they will try to score. The task can also be performed on different types of surfaces (e.g., turf, dirt) while on declined and inclined ramps, depending on the main task aim (power, maximum speed).

Task Material

2 flat markers; 2 small goals; 2 soccer balls; 2 weights (from 1 to 5 kg); different types of balls

The Thief

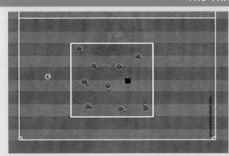 

Aim	Develop ability to stay on the ball under body restrictions		
Number of Players	**Pitch Size**	**Duration / Repetitions**	**Rest**
From 4 to 10 players	15×20 m	3-sets/3-reps (1 rep = sprinting with the weight, pick the ball and shoot to target)	1-min

Task Description

In a square, the players with the soccer ball (referred to as the hostages) must run away from the player without the ball (referred to as the thief). During the drill, the thief will try to steal the ball (referred to as the treasure) from the hostages. However, the hostages must travel with and stay on the ball under restricted body movements that are defined by the thief (e.g., both hands holding the ears, as seen in the right-hand side figure). When the thief steals the ball, a new thief is assigned, which will add a new movement restriction. That is, every time a new thief is assigned, he will introduce a different way of moving until he recovers another ball.

Adding Variability

Decrease space or use different types of pitches (circles, triangular, or wave-based pitches; for reference, search for "puckelball pitch in Malmö"). Increase the number of thieves. When working with youth players, the coach may make the task more interactive by including dice whose faces will have pictures correlating to specific themes that will assist the thief in creating different movements (e.g., superheroes, wild animals, professions).

Task Material

4 markers; 10 soccer balls; 1 bib

Minesweeper

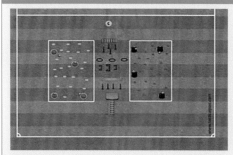 

Aim	Develop coordinative movement patterns and ability to travel with the ball under limited body movements		
Number of Players	**Pitch Size**	**Duration / Repetitions**	**Rest**
From 8 to 16 players	30×20 m	~6 min	1 min/bout 2 min/set

Task Description

In this game, players will travel with the soccer ball in the surrounding area based on the coach's instructions (e.g., only right foot, only left foot, alternate touches, low position; right right left left), while avoiding the "mines" on the ground (i.e., the markers). After the signal (either visual or sound), both teams should move between pitch areas using one of the different paths (they cannot repeat the same path while moving between zones). The first team to have all four players with a ball in the next pitch wins one point.

Adding Variability

Use different types of balls. Add more obstacles to the pitch. Instead of giving predefined paths, the players will have the possibility, using the available material between stations, to create their own type of movement between zones, where the only rule is to always be different. In addition, rather than traveling the ball, the teams may be challenged to pass between them without touching the "mines."

Task Material

As much material as possible to create different paths for the players (e.g., agility poles, wooden bench, tchoukballs, elastics connecting agility poles); 8 soccer balls; different color markers to simulate the mines

Hot Wheels

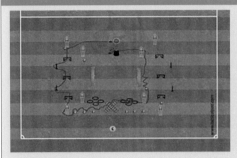 

Aim	Develop coordinative movement patterns and ability to travel with the ball under limited body movements

Number of Players	Pitch Size	Duration / Repetitions	Rest
From 2 to 8 players	30×20 m	2 sets / 3 reps (1 rep = performing the entire circuit one time)	1 min/bout 90 sec/set

Task Description

The players will start in a zone specified by a blue marker. Each player has their own path; however, they will cross in the middle of the circuit. The pitch has two zones for fundamental movement skills and two zones for game skills. After the signal (either visual or sound), the player must accelerate, pick the soccer ball, pass it under the hurdle, and run around the agility pole. After passing the ball under the last hurdle, he will leave the ball and run to the cones and jump over them.

After jumping the cones, the player will move through the agility ladder by skipping. To move through the ladder, the player places the right foot (1 step), then both feet (2 steps), and then the left foot (1 step). In the final part, the ball must be passed three times to the wooden bench, before the player drops the ball and accelerates to the end the course.

Adding Variability

Perform the task using different types of balls (see right-hand side figure).

Task Material

6 hurdles; 2 wooden benches; 8 training mannequins; 8 training rings; 2 agility ladders; 6 cones; 2 markers; 2 soccer balls; 4 agility poles

The Battle

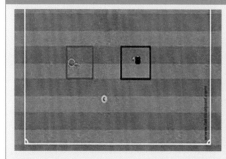 

Aim	Develop players' divergent thinking coupled with dribbling skills

Number of Players	Pitch Size	Duration / Repetitions	Rest
From 2 to 6 players	10×10 m	8 min~	1 min

Task Description

This task aims to develop players' ability to create new ways of dribbling. The player defined to start the task will have 10 seconds to think on one way to dribble, and after that time, he must show it to the opposing player(s). The second player will have another 10 seconds to develop his own dribble and show it to the player(s). The task ends when one of the players fails to create a new dribbling pattern (i.e., the same dribble cannot be repeated). Here, players are encouraged to think in different ways and to personalize their own feint movements and dribbles.

Adding Variability

Include materials that players can interact with while dribbling (e.g., hockey stick). To adjust the task difficulty, coaches may create competition with more groups (e.g., four players), allowing each player to perform for 10 seconds and then think for 30 seconds (during which time other players are showing their skills) to improvise the new movement.

Task Material

8 markers; 2 soccer balls

40 Passes

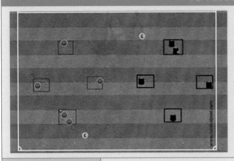 

Aim	Develop players' divergent thinking coupled with passing skills		
Number of Players	Pitch Size	Duration / Repetitions	Rest
5 players per team	10×10 m	2 sets/4 min (1 set = performing the 40 passes or maximum of 4 min)	1 min

Task Description

This task is performed in two groups, where there is one player in each square and two in the starting square. After the signal (either visual or sound), the player with the ball will pass the soccer ball to the next square in a clockwise order and follow the ball path to the next square. The player who received the ball will pass to the next station, and so on. However, the aim is to perform each pass in a different way. Only different passes are counted by the coach. The task ends when one team completes 40 passes (in different ways).

Adding Variability

Use other types of balls. Interlink the squares from both teams so that, in addition to having to pass in a different way, the players also have to adjust the pass according to their opponents' passing actions. Create themes for each square, where the pass must follow that theme (e.g., astronaut—the ball must be passed by the air, mammals—the ball must be passed with both arms and legs on the ground).

Task Material

32 markers; 2 soccer balls

The Great Wall

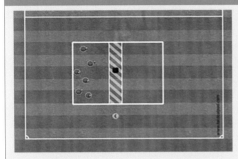 

Aim	Develop ability to travel with the ball		
Number of Players	**Pitch Size**	**Duration / Repetitions**	**Rest**
From 4 to 10 players	30×20 m	4 sets / 2 min (1 set = 2 min of the task)	1 min

Task Description

This game involves traveling with the soccer ball from zone A to B and crossing "the great wall," where there will be one defender who will try to steal the treasure (i.e., the ball) from the travelers. Players will have to travel with the ball in a way defined by either the coach or another player. If the defender steals the ball from a traveler, they will change their roles.

Adding Variability

Increase the number of defenders. Use different types of balls (see right-hand side figure). Increase task demands by having players perform it on a ramp (when moving up the ramp to cross the wall they will have to place more tension on the ball; when moving down the ramp, they will have to carefully adjust the tension to avoid losing the ball). Obstacles may also be added to limit the available space, and the players may interact with the obstacles to deceive the defender (e.g., search YouTube for the Messi video titled "hide and seek").

Task Material

Markers for the pitch boundaries; 1 bib; 10 soccer balls; different types of balls

The Sculptor

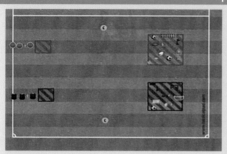 

Aim	Develop players' divergent thinking coupled with the ability to travel with the ball

Number of Players	Pitch Size	Duration / Repetitions	Rest
From 4 to 10 players	40 m long	~10 min	2 min

Task Description

After the signal (either visual or sound), the first player from each team will run to the designated spot, select one piece of the available material (i.e., for this task, all the available material can be used in as much as possible), return, and place it in the team box. The first player tags the next teammate's hand, and then that second player travels with the ball and repeats the task. Note that the second player must travel in a different way from the first player, and so on for each player. The task ends when either a team is unable to come up with a different way to travel with the ball or the time ends. The team that wins can select two extra materials. After, both teams have to design their own mascot using all the collected material, and the best wins the game..

Adding Variability

Travel with large balls (e.g., fitball). Include additional ball handling movements (e.g., dribble two balls [like you would a basketball] while traveling with the ball to pick up material). The material gathered might also be used by the players to create their own training exercises (e.g., design and test a warm-up for later sessions).

Task Material

Markers for the pitch boundaries; bibs; 10 soccer balls; different material (i.e., the coach must be as creative as possible in providing all type of material to their players).

Golf

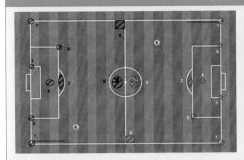 

Aim	Develop players' ability to control the ball in different ways		
Number of Players	**Pitch Size**	**Duration / Repetitions**	**Rest**
From 2 to 10 players	60×40 m	~12 min	1 min

Task Description

Two opposing players will have to place the ball in all nine holes (i.e., holes can be designated using training rings or flat markers that are placed in a circle shape to simulate real golf holes), and every touch on the ball should be performed in a new way (e.g., pick the ball with the hand, release it and pass it while falling, then pass it with the knee). The first player to get their ball into all nine holes wins. While being proposed as an individual task, coaches may decide to implement it in groups, where every player will touch the ball at a time (e.g., player A from blue team touches the ball and tries to put it closer to the hole, then player B from the same team, using a different movement, will try to place the ball in the hole or put it closer to the hole).

Adding Variability

Play with different ball types (see right-hand side figure). Create holes of varying sizes according to players' level of skill. Challenge players to put the ball inside the hole without doing it directly (i.e., using pitch material [e.g., rebounders] to place the ball inside the hole).

Task Material

1 ball per player; markers to create circles as the holes; different types of balls

The Way to Goal

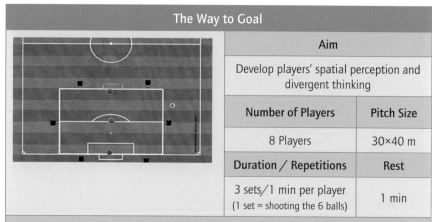

Aim	
Develop players' spatial perception and divergent thinking	
Number of Players	**Pitch Size**
8 Players	30×40 m
Duration / Repetitions	**Rest**
3 sets/1 min per player (1 set = shooting the 6 balls)	1 min

Task Description

One player stands in the middle of the pitch, which has two goalkeepers and six outside floaters. At the signal (either visual or sound), the player in the middle should adjust their body positioning to receive and score. The balls should be passed in different ways (e.g., faster, slower, high balls, bouncing balls). For each goal scored, the player is awarded one point. For shooting in a different way, the player is awarded two points. If the goal is scored in a different way, the player is awarded six points. After one minute, the player in the middle will switch places with one of the outside players. The player with the most points at the end of the set wins.

Adding Variability

Use different types of balls. Have the coach specify which target the player should aim for. Add obstacles (e.g., training mannequins) to increase difficulty while shooting at the goal or place markers on the ground surrounding the player so that his ball reception becomes more difficult.

Task Material

18 different types of balls; markers for the pitch boundaries; 2 regular goals

The Labyrinth

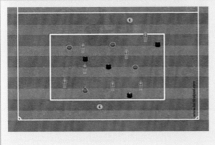

Aim	
Develop players' spatial perception and divergent thinking	
Number of Players	**Pitch Size**
From 2+2 to 5+5	30×40 m
Duration / Repetitions	**Rest**
2 sets / 4 min (1 set = performing the 50 passes)	1 min

Task Description

Players from each team will pass the ball between each other, attempting to perform a different type of pass each time (e.g., pass with the back, pass with the chest, pass with the shoulder). Points are awarded for every different pass. If the ball hits the training mannequin or opposing player, no point is awarded. The first team to complete 50 different passes wins.

Adding Variability

Use different types of balls. Include more obstacles. Promote dynamic spaces (increase or decrease the space of play). Task difficulty can be enhanced by two teams playing in a small playing area; two teams can play against each other and attempt to score in small goals (e.g., 4-a-side), while a third team can be added with the aim of passing the ball in different ways (without touching opponents or losing the ball) between the teammates, completing the 50 passes. Time is counted. When they finish, the teams change roles. Award 3 points for the team that passes the fastest, plus 1 extra point for every victory in the game (time ends when the team completes 50 passes).

Task Material

2 soccer balls; markers for the pitch boundaries; 7 training mannequins; 5 bibs; different types of balls

Fill the Basket (Go Shopping)

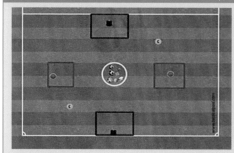 

Aim	Develop players' ability to travel with different types of balls		
Number of Players	Pitch Size	Duration / Repetitions	Rest
4 players	30×40 m	3 sets/2 min (1 set = all balls are at "home")	1 min

Task Description

This task is performed individually and is focused on traveling with the ball. After the signal (either visual or sound), players will accelerate to the middle, pick a ball, and bring it back to their own "house." Then, the players should return to the middle and retrieve another ball. When there are no more balls in the middle, the players should retrieve balls from their opponents' "houses." After two minutes, the player with the most balls wins. This task can also be done in teams. This task will not only cover the players' technical skills but will also enhance their conditioning, as it involves accelerating, decelerating, and traveling distances of varying lengths at distinct paces.

Adding Variability

Instead of using different balls, ask players to perform the task under different perceptual constraints (e.g., one foot wearing a tennis shoe and the other barefoot). The task can also be modified by selecting one team to catch the ball and place it in their "home" while, at the same time, the other team tries to steal it and place it back in the middle. When time is up, points are awarded based on the number of balls that a team has in their "house."

Task Material

Several different types of balls; 2 bibs; markers to set up the boundaries

The Snooker

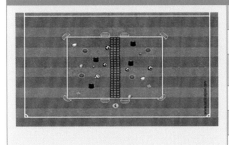

Aim	
Develop spatial awareness and ball control	
Number of Players	**Pitch Size**
8	30×20 m
Duration / Repetitions	**Rest**
2 sets / 4 min (1 set = scoring with all balls or after 4 min)	1 min

Task Description

This game (2vs2 + 2 NP for each team) is focused on developing players' perception of space and awareness of the movement covered by the ball in the air. To that end, each team has two players on each side, and several balls (of varying types) are spread out on the pitch, which is divided by a net (similar to volleyball). The goal is for a player on one side of the net to pass the ball through the air (players may choose how they wish to pass the ball [e.g., with the hands]) and a player from the same team on the opposite side to catch it. After catching the ball, the player should look to one target, release the ball, and kick it in the air to score. If the ball falls onto the ground, the receiving player can pick the ball and pass to the opposite side of the net to the first player (i.e., they change roles). The team that scores the most goals after all balls have been used would be considered the winner.

Adding Variability

Play with additional perceptual constraints (e.g., while wearing an eye patch). Instead of catching the ball, receive it with the foot. Require the players to kick at first touch, which would force them to pass the ball to different zones and also require the player who is kicking to adjust his body orientation. Add obstacles on the pitch to force the players to receive and adjust the kick to specific spaces. Divide the pitch into zones so that players are forced to receive or kick in different ways (based on the zone they are in).

Task Material

Several different types of balls; 4 bibs; 8 small goals; 1 net marker to set up the boundaries

Find a Home

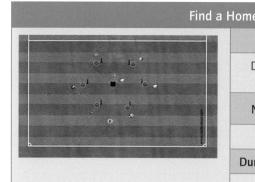

Aim	
Develop ability to travel with the ball under specific temporal pressure	
Number of Players	**Pitch Size**
7 players	15×15 m
Duration / Repetitions	**Rest**
3 sets/2 min (1 set = ends after 2 min)	1 min

Task Description

In this task, each player has a starting position defined by an agility pole (n=6) or training mannequin (n=1). in the training poles represent a "safe house" that can be awarded by arriving first to the house, while the training mannequin consists in the homeless. For the game, players must move from house to house for each repetition; players cannot be in the same house for two consecutive moves. The game starts when the homeless moves to find a home (i.e., moves to a training pole). All players in the houses must move to a different house with the soccer ball. The player that is not able to find a home loses and moves to the training mannequin (homeless). The player that travels to the training mannequin the least number of times wins.

Adding Variability

Include obstacles to challenge the players to adjust to the path (e.g., run around a training mannequin). Include perceptual constraints (e.g., one foot wearing a tennis shoe and the other barefoot). To increase task complexity, the same task can be performed with more groups (each having the same material), but instead of moving between the six homes from one group, the player can change to a different group (e.g., moving from group A to group B). To increase task complexity and place higher emphasis on coordination, require players to move through the route while dribbling a ball like they would a basketball or handball.

Task Material

6 agility poles; 1 training mannequin; 7 different types of balls

Sevbonaut

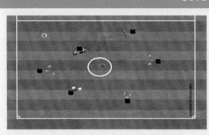

Aim	
Develop ability to control the ball within the space	
Number of Players	**Pitch Size**
7 players	15×15 m
Duration / Repetitions	**Rest**
2 sets/12 reps (1 rep = a pass from one of the 6 players)	1 min

Task Description

To start, one player will stand in the middle of a circle. Six players will be positioned around that player at different places and distances, and players will be identified by a specific code defined at every set (i.e., the coach will assign each player a code, such as numbers, nicknames, etc.). When the coach provides a signal (e.g., calling number 3), the player given that signal (e.g., in this case player number 3) will have to pass the soccer ball to the player in the middle. If the player in the middle is able to receive the ball within the circle, he will receive one point. Points are also awarded in relation to the number of touches: One touch equals three points; two touches equal two points; and three or more touches equal one point. The intention is for the player to be able to perceive the environment and adjust his body in a way that would allow him to receive the ball within the space with as few touches as possible.

Adding Variability

Use body restrictions instead of varying the type of ball (e.g., receiving the ball with both arms crossed in front of the chest). Add unstable surfaces for the player in middle. Create obstacles surrounding the circle so that when the ball hits them it changes trajectory. Similarly, to develop players' reaction speed, the zones surrounding the circle may be covered with specific material (e.g., towels stuck in agility poles) to make it more difficult for players to perceive from where the ball is coming, thereby making them more aware of their surroundings.

Task Material

14 balls (2 sets of 7 different types); markers for the circle

Me First!

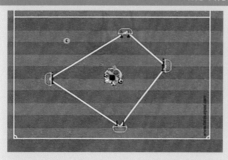 

Aim	Develop players' ability to travel with different types of balls		
Number of Players	Pitch Size	Duration / Repetitions	Rest
From 2 to 4 players	20×20 m	4 sets/3 reps (1 rep = picking one ball and scoring in the target)	1 min

Task Description

The players start in the middle of the circle. At the signal (either visual or sound), the players pick one ball from inside the same circle as their starting position and try to score while overcoming the obstacles that have been placed around the circle (e.g., cones in front of the goal, mannequins placed to create a labyrinth, etc.). The task can be performed individually, and the first player to score wins, or in teams, where the team whose two players score first would be considered the winner.

Adding Variability

Add body constraints (e.g., both arms crossed). Include perceptual constraints (e.g., wearing an eye patch). Goalkeepers can be assigned to the task, where two goalkeepers will try to defend the four targets, challenging the players to adjust their movements to score in one of the targets available. In addition, the task can also be performed on a 1vs1 basis (plus four neutral players). Upon the stimulus, the offensive player will pick the ball and try to score in one of the four targets, while the defender will press to try to prevent the offensive player from scoring.

Task Material

14 balls (2 sets of 7 different types); 8 agility poles; markers for the pitch boundaries

Tic-Tac-Toe

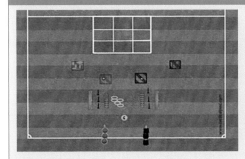 

Aim	Develop coordinative movement patterns		
Number of Players	Pitch Size	Duration / Repetitions	Rest
From 6 to 10 players	40×30 m	2 sets / 3 reps (1 rep = when one team wins by having 3 bibs in a row)	30 sec / bout 90 sec / set

Task Description

The task is performed individually in a relay race format. It is similar to the well-known Tic-Tac-Toe game. However, before placing a bib in the respective square, the first player from each column will have to choose a route (one: balance above the wooden bench; two: slalom between agility poles; three: skip in the speed ladder; four: jump on the training rings), then pick the soccer ball, travel with it to pick up a bib, place it on a square, and return as fast as possible to place the ball back in the starting position. Finally, they will accelerate to touch a teammate's hand, and that player will repeat the path, choosing a different number route (e.g., if the first player chose route one, the second should select route two).

Adding Variability

Instead of using the soccer ball, players can use other types of balls.

Task Material

10 training rings; 2 speed ladders; 6 agility poles; 2 benches; two squares; 10 bibs (2 different colors; 5 of one color and 5 of another); markers for boundaries

The Coach		
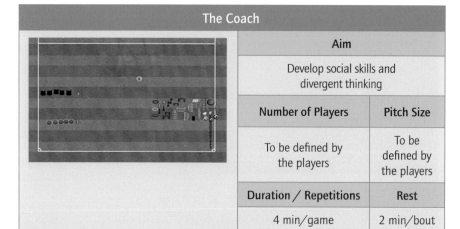	Aim	
	Develop social skills and divergent thinking	
	Number of Players	Pitch Size
	To be defined by the players	To be defined by the players
	Duration / Repetitions	Rest
	4 min/game	2 min/bout

Task Description

The game will start with a relay race, where the first player from each team will accelerate, pick up two pieces of material, and return to touch a teammate's hand. Then, the second player will accelerate and pick up two more pieces of material, and so on. The idea is to be faster than the other teams in order to select the best materials. In the end, each team will have to use the material they collected to create a game-based situation, show it to the opposing team, and then play that game against them. When picking up the material, the players must travel with a soccer ball.

Adding Variability

Players can pick up the material using groups of two to three, and the material cannot be caught with the hands (i.e., while in the first condition (see task description) players travel with the ball and carry the material in their hands; the purpose of this progression is that they explore new ways to travel with the material without using their hands).To increase game difficulty as well as fun, ask players to pick a card before traveling with the ball to pick up the material; the card will contain a theme pertaining to how they should travel with the ball. When doing this task with youth players, consider giving a theme to each team, and during a specific period of time (e.g., two minutes), the players will have to accelerate, pick up the material, and return. At the end of the designated period, they must use the material to highlight features of their theme. The design closest to the theme will win.

Task Material

There is no specific material. The main aim is to provide as many different and varied objects as possible so that the players can develop their divergent thinking.

Meso-Level Tasks (Individual Level)

Game of Thrones

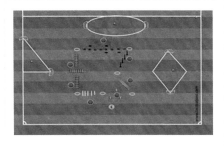

Aim

Develop players' movement coordination patterns and 1vs1 skills

Number of Players	Pitch Size
From 6 to 8 players	12×15m

Duration / Repetitions	Rest
2 sets / 4 min (1 set = 4-min, allowing different 1v1 and moves on the circuit)	2 min

Task Description

This task consists of a circuit that the players perform while music (or another sonorous stimulus) is playing. Once the music (or other stimulus) stops, players should run for the training rings (each training ring represents one kingdom) and stay inside the ring (i.e., this game is based on musical chairs, where participants move in a circle and when the music stops they attempt to sit on an available chair). When the music restarts, the players should continue the circuit. The game has two phases: 1) moving in the circuit, and when the music stops, being able to stop inside a training ring (1 point for each stoppage, if a player fails to stop inside the ring when the music stops, he is not awarded any points); 2) when the music changes; then the players must move to one of the are three differently shaped pitches (circle, square, triangle) , and they play 1vs1 to maintain ball possession until the music changes again, when they return to the circuit (when the music changes, the player with possession is awarded one point). With the 1v1 format, only six players can be in one of the three pitches; the two players that failed to arrive first to a pitch must continually bounce the ball in the air while the other players are performing the 1v1. Conditions can be adjusted according to the ages of the players.

Adding Variability

Play with different types of balls.

Task Material

As much material (e.g., cones, hurdles, training poles, training mannequins, wooden benches, etc.) as possible to create different paths for the players; 8 soccer balls; 6 small goals; 6 training rings; markers for the pitch boundaries; different types of balls

Big Head

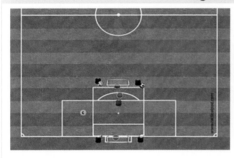

Aim	Develop players' heading skills		
Number of Players	**Pitch Size**	**Duration / Repetitions**	**Rest**
8 players	30×20 m	6 sets/45 sec (1 set = 45 sec, each player performs 2×45 sec)	15 sec/bout

Task Description

This game is played as Gk+1vs1+Gk + 2NP. One inside player is assigned as an attacker, and the other as a defender. The attacker moves to start the game. The attacker attempts changes of direction to try and deceive the defender while moving toward the opponent's goal. Two neutral players are at the endline with a ball (i.e., each floater has a different type of ball); when signaled to by the attacker, that neutral player throws the ball at the attacker's head so he can shoot to the target. If the attacker scores a goal, he is awarded with a new opportunity to attack. The attacker will now move to the opposing goal where there are two more neutral players waiting to pass the ball so the attacker can play a header. The defender will keep defending until the time ends or the attacker fails to score. If the attacker fails to score, then both players switch roles.

Adding Variability

Use different types of balls (see right-hand side figure). Add more targets (e.g., four targets, two at each side). Play with different pitch obstacles.

Task Material

2 regular goals; markers for the external boundaries; 3 bibs; 12 different types of balls

Monoball

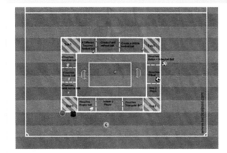 

Aim	Develop the ability to control the ball in tight spaces		
Number of Players	**Pitch Size**	**Duration / Repetitions**	**Rest**
2 to 6 players	40×30 m	~8 min	1 min / bout

Task Description

This game is similar to the board game Monopoly. However, in this version, each house has a different challenge (e.g., a specific number of touches with different balls). If the player is able to finish the challenge, he can move forward the next time that he throws the dice; however, if he fails to complete the challenge, he must wait for the opponent's move to be able to try again. Three houses will be considered as "1vs1," where the player will perform a 1vs1 challenge in the middle of the pitch, and the player who scores will be able to throw the dice twice. To win the game, the player must complete a specific number of rounds or finish all challenges (crossing all zones).

Adding Variability

Include different types of balls (see right-hand figure).

Task Material

7 different types of balls; 2 soccer balls; 1 balloon; 2 small targets cards; dice; markers for the pitch boundaries

Daredevil

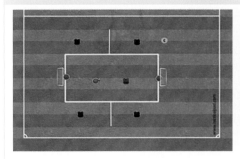 

Aim	Develop 1vs1 skills with increased perceptual demands		
Number of Players	Pitch Size	Duration / Repetitions	Rest
8 players	30×20 m	9 sets / 45 sec (1 set = 45 sec, each player performs 3×45 sec)	15 sec/bout

Task Description

This game is played as Gk+1vs1+Gk + 2NP and performed with perceptual manipulations that will change at every bout (e.g., playing barefoot [see right-hand side figure], playing with one foot wearing a tennis shoe and the other barefoot, playing with an eye patch, playing with a plastic bag covering the tennis shoe). The player in possession can use the neutral players as support. After 45 seconds, both players will stop the game and change roles with two of the neutral players.

Adding Variability

Use different types of balls. Integrate different material or obstacles (e.g., tchoukball). Design two pitches in the same space (i.e., one set up laterally, the other longitudinally); players play 1vs1 in each pitch with various materials added as obstacles during play.

Task Material

2 regular goals; markers for the external boundaries; 3 bibs; 6 soccer balls

AMGAP (As Many Goals As Possible)

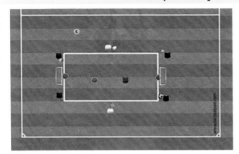 

Aim	Develop 1vs1 skills		

Number of Players	Pitch Size	Duration / Repetitions	Rest
10 players	20×25 m	6 sets / 45 sec (1 set = 45 sec, each player performs 2×45 sec)	15 sec/bout

Task Description

The game is played as Gk+1vs1+Gk + 4NP. To begin, one player is assigned as attacker. This player must play against a defender; he is supported by four neutral players (two are placed laterally on the pitch, and the other two at the endline). Each neutral player has a different type of ball. To develop offensive situations, the attacker may ask for one ball from one of the four neutral players. If the ball comes from one neutral player positioned at the endline, the attacker must shoot after only one touch on the ball; if he asks the ball from one of the lateral neutral players, he can play normally (i.e., without a set number of allowed touches). When the ball goes out of play (goal scored, goalkeeper catch or out of play), both players change roles. After 45 seconds (one repetition), they will change roles with two neutral players.

Adding Variability

Vary the ball types, sizes, weights, and shapes. Variation difficulty can be determined by the way a regular ball is passed (e.g., height, bounce, speed).

Task Material

2 regular goals; markers for the external boundaries; 5 bibs (3 of one color and 2 of another); different types of balls (e.g., swiss ball, reflex ball, tennis ball, rugby ball, plastic ball, etc.)

The Contortionist

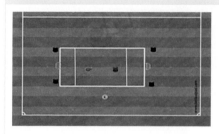

Aim	
Develop 1vs1 skills	
Number of Players	**Pitch Size**
6 players	15×20 m
Duration / Repetitions	**Rest**
9 sets / 45 sec (1 set = 45 sec, each player performs 3×45 sec)	15 sec/bout

Task Description

This game is played as a 1vs1 + 4 NP, performed with body constraints (i.e., specific body movements that will constrain the players' actions) that will change at every shot (e.g., playing with both hands on the chest, playing with both hands tied, playing with both hands holding the shorts, playing while holding another ball. playing with the right arm in abduction). The player in possession can use the neutral players as support. After 45 seconds, the two inside players will change roles with two of the neutral players. Assign different colors to the two teams (the blue player will link with the two blue neutral players, while the red player will link with the two red neutral players). The team with the most goals scored in the nine bouts wins.

Adding Variability

Use different types of balls. The player who concedes a goal then constrains the opposing player's movement by defining how he should move. Determine the way that players are constrained by using cards with specific themes that provide clues regarding how players should move or act (e.g., mummy-based movement).

Task Material

2 small goals; markers for the external boundaries; 3 bibs; 10 soccer balls; different types of balls

The Marriage

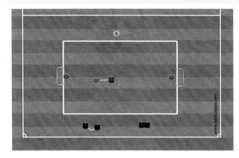 

Aim		Develop 1vs1 skills under varied distance to the opponent	
Number of Players	**Pitch Size**	**Duration / Repetitions**	**Rest**
4 players	15×20 m	9 sets / 30 sec (1 set = 30 sec, each player 3×30 sec)	30 sec / bout

Task Description

This task puts players in 1vs1 situations (i.e., Gk+1vs1+Gk) where they are tethered in some way to their opponent (e.g., by holding hands, tied with an elastic band), which teaches them to adapt their movement patterns during the game in relation to both distance and the opponent's actions. In this perspective, the coach may define three types of connection between players so that every player experiences one set using one of the connections. This will challenge the players to explore different solutions to creating space that would lead to goal scoring opportunities.

Adding Variability

Use rigid material (e.g., agility poles, ropes) or more variable material (e.g., elastic bands) to allow for variation in the distance between players. Adding pitch obstacles may also allow players to explore how to create space using the material as obstacles.

Task Material

2 regular goals; markers for the external boundaries; 3 bibs; 10 soccer balls; elastic band, agility poles, or rope

The Challenge

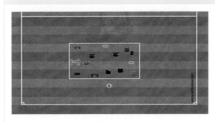

Aim	
Develop 1vs1 skills	
Number of Players	**Pitch Size**
From 6 to 8 players	20×25 m
Duration / Repetitions	**Rest**
5 reps / 30 sec (1 rep = 30 sec of 1vs1)	15 sec/bout

Task Description

In this task, several 1vs1 situations are performed simultaneously. Each player will be assigned a specific way of scoring (e.g., below hurdles, in the middle of training rings, inside a box, in a hole placed between training mannequins) that will vary at every bout. That is, during the first bout, player A and B score below the hurdles, then in the second bout, the same players will score by putting the soccer ball in the training ring, then in the third bout by placing the ball in the hole in the training mannequins. The task can be performed by one player scoring in one target and the opponent in the other or by both scoring on the same target. Points can be awarded by each goal scored, and if a player scores in all different targets in the game, extra points can be awarded.

Adding Variability

In addition to the different types of targets, coaches may also add different types of balls. Consider including body restrictions. Despite being 1vs1, the task may also be performed in groups (e.g., 3vs3) where there is only one ball in play and two teams facing each other. A specific target can be assigned to both teams, or each player from each team can be assigned a different type of target to score.

Task Material

2 hurdles; 2 training rings; 2 boxes; 2 training mannequins (or basketball baskets); coaches may design other ways of scoring that allows the ball to hit the target; 8 soccer balls

Ruined House

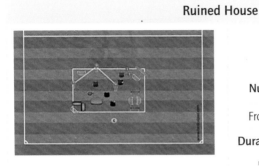

Aim

Develop 1vs1 skills

Number of Players	Pitch Size
From 6 to 8 players	20×25 m

Duration / Repetitions	Rest
5 reps / 30 sec (1 rep = 30 sec of 1vs1)	15 sec/bout

Task Description

This task consists of various 1vs1 exercises, where the players perform in a pitch with a considerable number of obstacles (e.g., training mannequins tethered together by an elastic band, cones, wooden bench, hurdles, boxes, mattress). Players should interact with these obstacles to dribble around the opponent and score as many goals as possible. When a goal is scored, the player who conceded the goal will restart the game from that goal. However, he cannot score in that target during that possession. This intends to simulate street soccer, where the players interact with their surroundings (e.g., trees) to hide and seek (as previously mentioned in the Messi video), allowing them to create space. Similarly, during these street games, it is common to see players using the wall as a bouncer to overcome an opponent. Under this perspective, this task intends to recreate those scenarios and create freedom for the players to explore their environment.

Adding Variability

Combine with perceptual constraints (e.g., wearing an eye patch, playing barefoot). Consider including body restrictions.

Task Material

5 small goals; 1 mattress; 3 training mannequins; 1 elastic band; 2 boxes; 2 cones; 1 wooden bench; 2 hurdles; 8 soccer balls

Wrestling

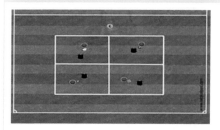

Aim	
Develop ability to stay on the ball	
Number of Players	**Pitch Size**
Total of 8 players	40×40 m
Duration / Repetitions	**Rest**
8 sets/15 sec (1 set = 15 sec holding/ shielding the ball)	15 sec/bout

Task Description

This task is performed 1vs1 in four different squares. To start, the coach will define the player in possession (first attacker) from each square. Then, and after the signal (either visual or sound), the player in possession must maintain possession of the soccer ball (i.e., stay on the ball) for a period of 15 seconds. If the player is able to maintain possession of the ball within the square during this period, he will be awarded three points. However, he will lose one point for every time the ball goes out of the square. If the defending player is holding the ball when the time is up, he will be awarded two points. In the next set, the two players will change roles (i.e., the player that first defended will now attack).

Adding Variability

Combine with different body restrictions (e.g., hands crossed on the chest, both arms up, hands holding a ball). Add obstacles on the pitch to increase players' interaction with it. Also, the game may start with both players passing to each other (e.g., through the air), and at the stimulus (either visual or sound), the player with the ball will have to put it down and protect it (increasing task difficulty).

Task Material

4 bibs; markers for the pitch boundaries; 4 different types of balls

Hockey Game

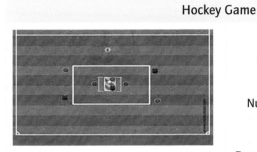

Aim

Develop spatial awareness and
1vs1 skills

Number of Players	Pitch Size
6 players	30×20 m

Duration / Repetitions	Rest
9 sets / 45 sec (1 set = 30 sec, or 2 ball possessions; 3 sets performed per player)	15 sec/bout

Task Description

This game starts with both players in the middle of the pitch in a specified zone. To begin, one player will be assigned as the attacker, and the other will be assigned as the defender. The 1vs1 starts when the offensive player decides to touch the soccer ball, allowing the defender to become active. Once the game starts, the player in possession can attack both goals and also has the opportunity to link with one of the two neutral players belonging to his team (e.g., blue player can link with blue neutral players, red player can link with neutral red players). If the defending player recovers the ball, the roles change (the defending player becomes the attacker, and the other player becomes the defender). The game lasts for a duration of 45 seconds or two ball possessions. The first ball possession allows one player (e.g., blue player) to attack. If he scores, the game restarts in the same zone with the ball from the red player. If he loses the ball and the red player scores a goal, then the red player will take possession (so each player has an opportunity to start with the ball in the central zone).

Adding Variability

Perform using different types of balls. It is also possible to create a more dynamic game, where, once the ball is passed to a neutral player, he will turn into the game, and the player that passes to him will replace him as neutral player. This can be done by teams and increasing the total task time.

Task Material

2 regular goals; 3 bibs; markers for the pitch boundaries; 6 soccer balls; different types of balls

Be Like Xavi (Hernandez)

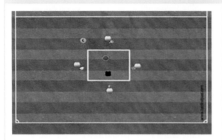

Aim	
Develop passing skills	
Number of Players	**Pitch Size**
6 players	10×10 m
Duration / Repetitions	**Rest**
6 sets/30 sec (1 set = 30 sec; each player performs 2 sets)	1 min/bout

Task Description

For 30 seconds, the player assigned as attacker (blue), will try to use the neutral players (1vs1+4 NP) to receive and pass the ball as many times as possible, while the defender (red) will try to intercept and avoid the passes. The neutral players have different types of balls. The ball should be passed when the attacker asks for it. The pass is only counted if the ball arrives at its destination and the defender did not touch on it. After 30 seconds, both players get out and perform as neutral players, while two others will participate in the exercise. This task is focused on power, as the continuous changes-of-direction will create momentary fatigue in players. The task can be performed under two perspectives: individually, to see which players performed more passes than all players; or group-based, where the two teams are competing each other (e.g., blue player #1 = 6 passes; blue player #2 = 9 passes; blue player #3 = 7 passes; blue team = 22 passes).

Adding Variability

This is an intense task, so coaches may begin with 15 to 20 second durations. Additionally, body restrictions may be added to increase task complexity.

Task Material

3 bibs; different types of balls (i.e., at least 8 different types); markers for the pitch boundaries

The Bounce

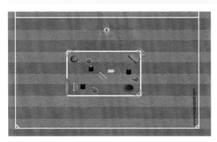

Aim

Develop 1vs1 skills

Number of Players	Pitch Size
From 6 to 8 players	30×20 m

Duration / Repetitions	Rest
4 sets/30 sec (1 set = 30 sec of 1vs1)	30 sec/bout

Task Description

Different pairs will perform 1vs1 situations in which the players have to interact with the material to score – the goal is only attributed if the ball bounces in the material and goes to the goal (e.g., use the wooden bench to score or the tchoukball). One point is awarded for each goal scored. After scoring, the game is restarted by the player who conceded the goal, who cannot score in the same target in that attempt (due to close distance). This task challenges the players to explore all available possibilities to score, as they are required to create that same goal-scoring opportunities by interacting with the material available. Can be developed an a 1vs1 or separated by teams (e.g., 4vs4).

Adding Variability

Vary the type, shape, and size of goals used. Recreate this task in pitches with slopes (e.g., the player to score must kick the ball to the slope, and after going down the slope, enter in the target). Perceptual demands, such as playing with an eye patch, may also increase the number of opportunities to explore the goal situations (mainly at group level, 4vs4).

Task Material

3 to 4 bibs; 4 soccer balls; wooden bench; 5 small goals; 1 tchoukball; 1 trampoline; 1 mattress; 1 balance trainer

Jigsaw

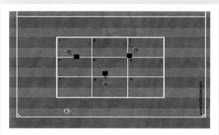

Aim	
Develop 1vs1 skills	
Number of Players	**Pitch Size**
From 6 to 8 players	30×30 m
Duration / Repetitions	**Rest**
6 sets/15 sec (1 set = 15 sec of 1vs1; each player performs 2 sets)	15 sec/bout

Task Description

Players have to maintain possession by dribbling to the opponent or staying on the ball for 15-second periods. The pitch will be divided into zones; each zone has different rules: 1) only weak foot; 2) alternate between right and left touch; 3) only roll over the ball; 4) move with the ball backwards; 5) free (i.e., player can decide how to move the ball); 6) only touch the ball with external part of the foot; 7) play ball in the air only; 8) only inside part of the foot; 9) three-touch zone. If a player breaks a rule, the ball will be given to the defender. Every 15 seconds, the coach gives a sound signal to end the task, and a point is awarded to the player in possession. Note that if the ball leaves a zone, the game restarts, but the defender has the ball and becomes the attacker.

Adding Variability

Use different body constraints in each box. Add pitch obstacles to increase players' interactions and allow them to create more space to stay on the ball. The task can be upgraded for a group-based game (e.g., 3vs3), where every time a player touches the ball, he must move to a different zone before he can touch the ball again.

Task Material

3 to 4 bibs; 4 soccer balls; papers with rules or written with paint; markers for the pitch boundaries; different types of balls

Catch the Man

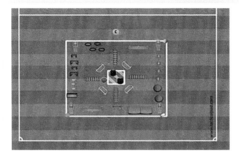 

Aim	Develop coordinative movement patterns		
Number of Players	**Pitch Size**	**Duration / Repetitions**	**Rest**
5 players	30×20 m	sets / 3 min (1 set = 3 min or player scoring in the small goal)	1 min bout / 2 min set

Task Description

This task begins with the blue player moving from the center zone. However, he can only move between the zones with material (e.g., by starting from the middle, he should use one of the four agility ladders to progress). After he touches the first ball, one defender will begin chasing him. Then, after touching the second ball, the second defender will start to chase him. The blue player is attempting to place the four balls on the four corners and score them in the four pop-up goals while the defenders (the red players) try to touch him. If they touch him, all players come to the middle, but in the second attempt, the defender will leave as soon as the attacker crosses the agility ladder. Each player has a maximum of three attempts. In the third, he will be chased by the two players (the first defender leaves once he finishes the agility ladder, the second, when the first defender crosses the agility ladder – to allow time for the attacker to move).

Adding Variability

Leave three different types of balls in the central square, and each player must find a way to travel with one of the balls within the stations.

Task Material

As much material as possible to create different paths for the players (e.g., agility poles, wooden benches, tchoukball, cones, markers, hurdles, etc.); 4 different types of balls; 4 agility ladders

The Handkerchief

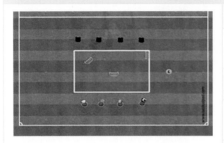

Aim	
Develop ability to kick with varied tension and precision	
Number of Players	**Pitch Size**
1vs1 (4 players per team)	30×20 m
Duration / Repetitions	**Rest**
4 sets / 1 min (1 set = 1 rep of 1vs1 or other play variation)	30 sec / bout

Task Description

Each player will be given a different number (one through four) and type of ball. For that purpose, one team will start as the attacking team, the other as the defending team. When the coach says a number, the corresponding attacker and defender will face each other on the pitch, and the attacker will try to score a goal while the defender attempts to recover the ball. In each set, the team that attacks and defends changes. Players' numbers should be changed prior to each set so they are facing different opponents during each bout.

Adding Variability

Include different scoring methods or only allow goals if scored in a different way (e.g., if a player scores a goal with a bicycle kick, no other player can use a bicycle kick to score). Call more than one player per team and allow players to score with either one of the balls or both (i.e., if each attacker has his own ball, then when two attackers are called, there will be two balls in play at the same time). To change the signal from sound to visual, players may wear different colored bibs, and when the coach shows a color, the players wearing that color will perform the 1vs1.

Task Material

4 bibs; 4 different types of balls; 3 small goals; markers for the pitch boundaries

Picasso

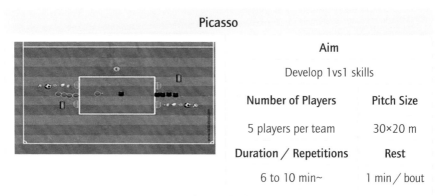

Aim

Develop 1vs1 skills

Number of Players	Pitch Size
5 players per team	30×20 m

Duration / Repetitions	Rest
6 to 10 min~	1 min / bout

Task Description

To start, each team will pick a card with a picture on it that represents the drawing that the team has to design. The game starts with a 1vs1. When a goal is scored, the player who scores will leave the pitch and be replaced by a teammate. The player that scored will then leave the game to move to the table and add a line to his team's drawing. After the goal, it is the opposing team's turn to try to create goal-scoring situations. After every goal, the game restarts with a different type of ball. Also, if a player concedes two consecutive goals without scoring, he is replaced by a teammate and will not be able to add a line to his team's design. The first team to complete their drawing would be considered the winner.

Adding Variability

Add obstacles that might help the players to explore new opportunities for action or use tchoukballs, where scoring a goal is only possible by using it to score (i.e., the ball hits the tchoukball that acts as rebounder and guides the ball to the goal). Integrate with perceptual constraints (e.g., wearing an eye patch, playing barefoot, wearing only one tennis shoe).

Task Material

5 bibs; 8 different balls; 4 small goals; 2 tables; colored pencils; markers for the pitch boundaries

93

Multisport Game

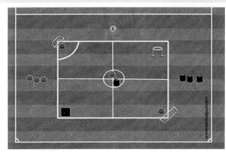 

Aim	Develop 1vs1 skills		
Number of Players	**Pitch Size**	**Duration / Repetitions**	**Rest**
4 players per team	40×40 m	4 sets / 45 sec (1 set = 45 sec of 1vs1 or 2 ball possessions)	15 sec / bout 1 min / set

Task Description

This game starts with a 1vs1 in the middle of the circle. The soccer ball is given to one player, who can score in one of the four targets ([1] regular goal defended by goalkeeper, [2] 5-a-side target defended by a goalkeeper and goal scored using handball rules, [3] hole (e.g., using a box), goal scored by placing the ball inside of it, [4] basketball basket, goal scored by shooting like in basketball. If the first player in possession scores, the ball will be given to the defending player, and the game will restart in the middle. If the defender steals the ball, he can attempt to score, and the game will restart with his ball possession. After two attempts of a maximum of 45 seconds, both players come out, and the other two will go in. Each goal equals one point. Scoring in all targets equals four extra points.

Adding Variability

Use different types of balls. Create a labyrinth with obstacles for the players to interact with. Play with two teams of four with one player in each square.

Task Material

4 bibs; 6 soccer balls; 1 small goal; 1 regular goal; 1 basketball basket (or similar); 1 box; markers for the pitch boundaries

Meso-Level Tasks (Group Level)

Two Balls Game

Aim	Develop players' breadth of attention		
Number of Players	Pitch Size	Duration / Repetitions	Rest
10 players	40×30 m	2 sets of 4 min (1 set = 4 min)	1 min / bout

Task Description

This game is played as a Gk+5vs5+Gk with two soccer balls at the same time. Each goalkeeper will start the game with a ball. Players are challenged to develop strategies to maintain possession and recover the other ball (if they have only one) or to develop offensive strategies that allow them to attack with both balls without losing them. After a goal or ball is out of play, the goalkeeper from the team who has possession restarts the game. This type of task requires players to have a wider breadth of attention to sustain both offensive and defensive actions.

Adding Variability

Every time a ball goes out of play, the game can be restarted with a different type of ball. To start with an easier progression, coaches may divide the pitch into two corridors, where two to three players per team play on each side (e.g., left corridor 2vs2, right corridor 3vs3, each zone with a ball).

Task Material

2 regular goals; markers to define boundaries; 5 bibs; 10 soccer balls; different types of balls

Three Balls Game

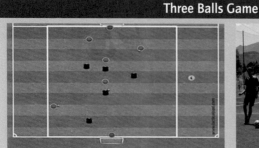

Aim	Develop players' strategic thinking and breadth of attention		
Number of Players	**Pitch Size**	**Duration / Repetitions**	**Rest**
12 players	40×30 m	3 sets of 4 min (1 set = 4-min game)	2 min / bout

Task Description

This game is played as a Gk+5vs5+Gk, with one player from each team holding a soccer ball in his hands. The game is played normally; however, when the player in possession catches the ball from the ground with his hands, the corresponding teammate that initially held the ball must place his ball on the ground. For example, if A1 has the ball and A4 catches the ball from the ground, A1's ball becomes the game ball. In this respect, all teams always have the game ball plus one additional ball held by a teammate. that additional ball comes into play when his team has possession and the ball is caught from the ground. It is important to note that the player holding the ball can normally interact with the ball on the ground; however he cannot catch it while holding the other ball. This is a strategy game, as with only one movement the players are able to catch the ground ball or, instead, catch and release it until a teammate becomes free. Therefore, players are invited to explore as much as possible the game rules.

Adding Variability

The ball being carried in the hands can be a different one (e.g., blue team rugby ball; red team triangular shape ball).

Task Material

2 regular goals; markers to define boundaries; 5 bibs; 3 soccer balls; different types of balls

Twins

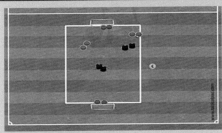 

Aim	Develop movement adaptability		
Number of Players	Pitch Size	Duration / Repetitions	Rest
10 players	20×30 m	2 sets / 3 min (1 set = 3 min game)	2 min / bout

Task Description

In this game (Gk+5vs5+Gk), players are connected (e.g., by holding hands) to a teammate (e.g., using the Gk+1:3:1 playing system, the central defender may play tethered to the central defender, the right midfielder to the center midfielder, and the left midfielder to the striker). This game challenges the players to perform with dynamic body restrictions, as each player movement should be coupled with the movement of his teammate.

Adding Variability

Rather than be connected to a teammate, players can be connected to an opponent (see right-hand side figure). Instead of holding hands, players may also be connected with different types of material (e.g., rope, elastic bands).

Task Material

2 regular goals; markers to define boundaries; 5 bibs; 10 soccer balls

Storytelling

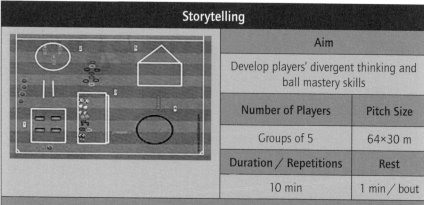

Aim	
Develop players' divergent thinking and ball mastery skills	
Number of Players	Pitch Size
Groups of 5	64×30 m
Duration / Repetitions	Rest
10 min	1 min / bout

Task Description

In this task, items are placed on the ground to create different scenarios. Then, each group will be assigned their own scenario and will have to explore it. After that, the aim is for the players from each team to create a story using their scenario. Player one begins by verbalizing the story, and each of his teammates will then add on to it. For example, player one starts by saying, "we were at the school, and during breaks we played street soccer," player two says, "and when we finished, we went to the park to play 2vs2," player three says, "before going to our swim lesson, we went to a sport store," player four says, "to buy some balls to take to school. I bought two and dribbled them home," and player five finishes by saying, "and after swim class, I went home to play with my brother." The material positioned on the floor will serve as inspiration for the story, and the players must cover all material to create the story. Moving from section to section (i.e., using the previous example, moving from school to the park) must be done by traveling with the ball.

Adding Variability

Some players may act out the story without speaking, and the teammates have to guess what scenario is being represented (similar to the game Pictionary). Also, the coach may use specific dices or cards (i.e., cards that have themes or cartoons that will guide the players' divergent thinking). For example, one dice may have faces related to traveling, and so, showing different backgrounds, such as the jungle, the beach, the mountain, etc., that may inspire the players' story. Or cards that have players' pictures can be used as a priming strategy to guide how players should move and behave.

Task Material

Several materials that represent scenarios (e.g., wooden benches, cones, markers, flat markers, different goal sizes, hurdles, training rings, etc.)

In and Out

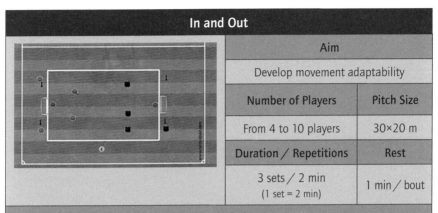

Aim	
Develop movement adaptability	
Number of Players	**Pitch Size**
From 4 to 10 players	30×20 m
Duration / Repetitions	**Rest**
3 sets / 2 min (1 set = 2 min)	1 min / bout

Task Description

This game consists of varying the number of available players. To that end, each player will be assigned a number. The game starts with a Gk+4vs4+Gk situation, and the coach will randomly call one to three players from each team with a difference of 10 seconds (e.g., in the 10th second, the coach says numbers two and four from team A, in the 20th second the coach says number one from team B, and so on), which will lead to removing or adding players to the game (e.g., if player one from team B is playing and his number is mentioned by the coach, then he must leave the pitch; if he is out and his number is mentioned, he will join the game). In this regard, at every 20 seconds there is a change on each team, and at every 10 seconds a change to the game. Under this perspective, players will be faced with different numerical relations that will require them to act according to the number of players (e.g., pressing in numerical superiority or defending closer to the goal when facing numerical inferiority).

Adding Variability

Play with different types of balls. Combine with pitch obstacles (e.g., wooden benches to recreate a cage or elastic bands connected between agility poles).

Task Material

4 agility poles; 8 soccer balls; 4 bibs; 2 regular goals; markers for the pitch boundaries; different types of balls

Abracadabra

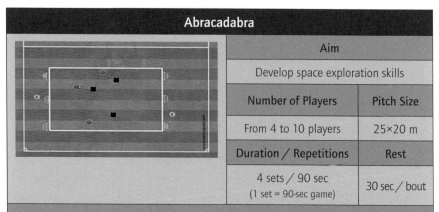

Aim	
Develop space exploration skills	
Number of Players	**Pitch Size**
From 4 to 10 players	25×20 m
Duration / Repetitions	**Rest**
4 sets / 90 sec (1 set = 90-sec game)	30 sec / bout

Task Description

This game is played 3vs3, where a coach behind each goal line will change and vary the number of goals available by placing a green bib in the targets that are available to score in. The available targets to score in will be changed on a 15-second basis. In this regard, the game can be played with (a) three targets per team, (b) two targets per team, (c) one target per team (in the corridor or central zone), (d) one target in the middle (team A) and the other in the corridor (team B), (e) diagonal targets, (f) one central target (team A) and two corridor targets (team B), (g) four corridor targets (team A) and two central targets (team B), or (h) both team A and B defending two goals at the corridors on their side plus the central goal on the opposing side.

Adding Variability

Manipulate goal sizes between bouts (e.g., pop-up goal, 5-a-side goal, 7-a-side goal, 11-a-side goal plus goalkeeper). Vary target orientation and angles. Vary the types of balls used.

Task Material

6 small goals; 9 bibs(6 green bibs that allow the coach to mark the goals that can be scored on and 3 bibs that are a different color to distinguish the players); 6 soccer balls; different types of balls

Hands and Feet

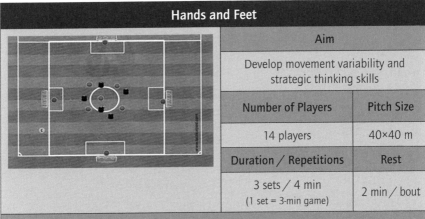

	Aim	
	Develop movement variability and strategic thinking skills	
	Number of Players	**Pitch Size**
	14 players	40×40 m
	Duration / Repetitions	**Rest**
	3 sets / 4 min (1 set = 3-min game)	2 min / bout

Task Description

This game is played with 4 goalkeepers vs 5vs5). The players can play with hands and feet at the same time. The players can score in all four targets defended each by a goalkeeper, and one point is awarded for scoring a goal with the hand outside the goalkeeper area, three points are awarded if the ball hits the training ring, one point is awarded for goals scored with the foot inside the goalkeeper area, two points are awarded for goals scored with the foot outside the goalkeeper playing area, and three points are awarded for goals scored with the foot inside the training rings. Each ball possession starts from the middle (center circle), and the player in possession can start by traveling with the ball or passing to a teammate.

Adding Variability

The coach may manipulate the rules so that each team defends or attacks two targets. Vary the types of balls used. Promote variation in the rules (e.g., in each pitch quarter, the players must play a specific type of sport).

Task Material

4 regular goals; 12 training rings; markers for the pitch boundaries and areas; 5 bibs; 6 soccer balls; different types of balls

Playground		
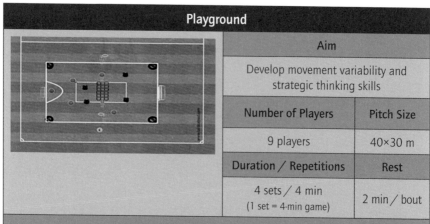	Aim	
	Develop movement variability and strategic thinking skills	
	Number of Players	Pitch Size
	9 players	40×30 m
	Duration / Repetitions	Rest
	4 sets / 4 min (1 set = 4-min game)	2 min / bout

Task Description

This is a multisport game played as a Gk+4vs4, where each team can score in the handball goal (using handball rules), in one of the four tires (by placing the ball inside), in the upper part of a regular goal (delimited with plastic tape or an elastic band), or in the two basketball baskets (using basketball rules). Each goal is equal to one point. In the middle there is a volleyball net, over which the players attempt to pass the ball, using their heads, to the opposite side; if the ball hits the ground, it equals one point. Scoring in all targets equals five points (i.e., scoring in the handball goal, regular target without goalkeeper, one of the basketball goals, one of the tires, and on the volleyball court). When a goal is scored, players begin from the closest corner of the pitch (player can pass or travel with the ball).

Adding Variability

Play with different body restrictions (e.g., right arm touching left knee). Add perceptual constraints (e.g., wearing an eye patch, playing barefoot).

Task Material

4 tires; 2 regular goals; 1 net; 2 basketball baskets; 4 bibs; 6 soccer balls; 3 wooden benches; markers for boundaries

The Signalman

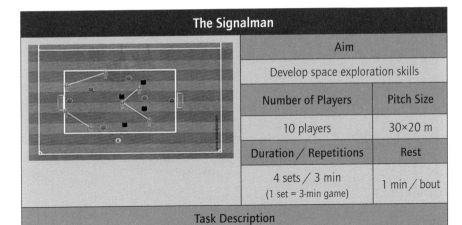

Aim	
Develop space exploration skills	
Number of Players	Pitch Size
10 players	30×20 m
Duration / Repetitions	Rest
4 sets / 3 min (1 set = 3-min game)	1 min / bout

Task Description

In this game, two teams compete (Gk+4vs4+Gk). Players will perform with obstacles on the pitch (e.g., training mannequins tethered together with elastic bands) to restrict space and challenge the players to explore other possible spaces and movement solutions. The elastic bands may be placed at different heights, so that some players have to jump over them, and other players have to move under them. For example, in one side of the pitch, spaces close to the corridor may be closed to force one team to attack by central zones while the other team faces the opposite configuration to force them to explore the corridors. It is important to note that the creation of such paths may allow the players to move from most sides, allowing them to use the positioning of these obstacles to their advantage to score goals.

Adding Variability

To increase task complexity, while two teams are playing and trying to score and deal with the training mannequins with the bands, another two teams are trying to maintain possession in the same space, creating additional variability in the task increasing the task perceptual demands). The task might also be performed in pitches with different surfaces, such as dirt, artificial turf, or sand.

Task Material

2 regular goals; 4 bibs; 7 training mannequins; 4 elastic bands; 6 soccer balls

The Sheriff

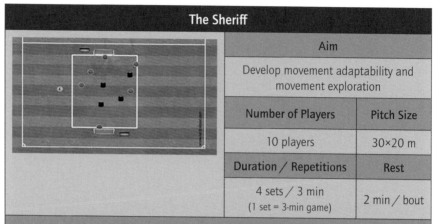

Aim	
Develop movement adaptability and movement exploration	
Number of Players	**Pitch Size**
10 players	30×20 m
Duration / Repetitions	**Rest**
4 sets / 3 min (1 set = 3-min game)	2 min / bout

Task Description

The purpose of this game (Gk+4vs4+Gk) is to create rules that will be applied to the team who conceded the goal. For that purpose, before the game, each team will define seven rules that will be attributed to the opposing team after each conceded goal. Players should be instructed that the rules cannot be linked to denying scoring or freezing the opponents' players; however, they can state that only a specific player may score. After establishing and writing the rules on a small sheet of paper, the game will start. When a player scores a goal, he will pick one of the papers and tell the opposing team how they should behave (e.g., playing holding hands; scoring goals only with the knee, moving in a snakelike way [i.e., all together, four touches mandatory per player]). When a team scores a goal, they may choose to apply the rule to the opposing team or cancel the current rule imposed by the opposing team (due to a goal they had conceded).

Adding Variability

Include training material for the players to interact with (e.g., use agility poles to simulate hockey and challenge the opposing team to pass the ball as they would in hockey).

Task Material

2 regular goals; markers for the pitch boundaries; 4 bibs; 6 soccer balls

Downhill

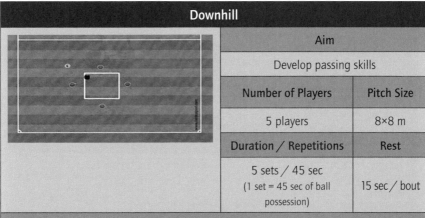

Aim	
Develop passing skills	
Number of Players	**Pitch Size**
5 players	8×8 m
Duration / Repetitions	**Rest**
5 sets / 45 sec (1 set = 45 sec of ball possession)	15 sec / bout

Task Description

This game is played 4vs1 in a declined rondo, and the player in the middle will change position when touching the ball or when an offensive player performs a bad pass (e.g., passing the soccer ball to outside of the playing zone). At every bout, a new player should start in the middle. Additionally, at every bout, all players should rotate clockwise, so they are exposed to all conditions. This task will develop players' ability to pass the ball with varying levels of power, which might be useful, for example, when playing in a pitch full of water (where players would have to explore different passing patterns).

Adding Variability

To increase task difficulty, vary the types of balls used. Alternatively, players maintaining possession might be tethered together (e.g., with elastic bands, forcing them to better control the passing actions). In addition to the slope, the pitch can be made of different surfaces (e.g., turf, dirt). Lastly, recreating the pitch on specific grounds (e.g., spaces where in the middle there is a tree or other obstacle), forcing the players to adapt their movement actions.

Task Material

6 soccer balls; 1 bib; markers for pitch boundaries; different types of balls

Seven Balls Game

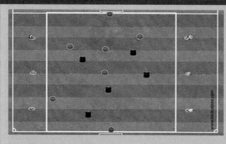 

Aim	Explore the creation of numerical superiorities and develop strategic thinking		
Number of Players	**Pitch Size**	**Duration / Repetitions**	**Rest**
12 players	30×20 m	2 sets / 3 min (1 set = 3-min game)	1 min / bout

Task Description

In this game (Gk+5v5+Gk), every time a ball goes out of play, it is replaced by another ball. When a team scores a goal, that scoring team will select one of the other six balls placed in the training rings and restart the game by traveling with the ball or attempting to pass it to one of the teammates (the goal scored will serve as the reward). The team who conceded the goal will have to use one of his players to pick the ball and place it in the empty training ring (remember that the team that scored the goal picked the ball from one of the training rings), and this player can only intervene in the match after placing the ball. However, to increase the game pace, if the team that scored and is awarded with a new ball scores again before the opposing team places the ball, the goal is equal to two points. However, during the game, if a team's shot misses the target and the ball goes out of play, the opposing team will select one of the balls from the training rings and begin play while the player that missed the shot must bring the ball.

Adding Variability

Vary the types of balls used.

Task Material

2 regular goals; markers for the pitch boundaries; 6 training rings; 5 bibs; 7 different types of balls

The Neighbor

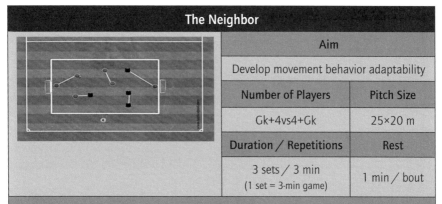

Aim	
Develop movement behavior adaptability	
Number of Players	**Pitch Size**
Gk+4vs4+Gk	25×20 m
Duration / Repetitions	**Rest**
3 sets / 3 min (1 set = 3-min game)	1 min / bout

Task Description

This exercise (Gk+4vs4+Gk) consists of playing under different conditions. That is, players will play the game while tethered to a teammate, goalkeeper, or opponent. For that purpose, a rope is given to each group of two players to maintain their connection. After each bout, the players should experiment with different type of connections (e.g., linking goalkeeper with an opposing player then linking him with the same team striker).

Adding Variability

Play with different types of balls to emphasize technical adaptability. Use pitch obstacles to increase space exploration. Rather than linking groups of two players, consider creating additional perturbations by linking two teammates with one opponent in the middle, which will amplify the exploration of strategic behaviors. The ropes may also be of different lengths to expose players to distinct interpersonal distances.

Task Material

6 soccer balls; 4 bibs; 5 ropes; markers for pitch boundaries; different types of balls

Castle Robbery

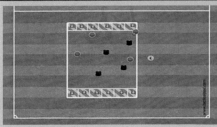 

Aim	Develop interpersonal coordination patterns		
Number of Players	Pitch Size	Duration / Repetitions	Rest
8 players	30×20 m	2 sets / 4 min (1 set = 4-min game)	1 min / bout

Task Description

The aim of this game (4vs4) is for the team in possession to hit the opponents' cones, each time in a different way (e.g., if the first cone is hit with the heel, the next one must be hit in a different way, such as with the knee). When a cone is hit, the team who hit it will win that cone and can then use it to create a barrier to protect their own cones. The first team to hit all the six cones wins.

Adding Variability

Promote the use of different types of balls (see right-hand side figure). Add perceptual variability (e.g., play with one foot using a boot and the other barefoot)

Task Material

Markers for the pitch boundaries and areas; 12 cones; 4 bibs; 3 soccer balls; different types of balls

Priming

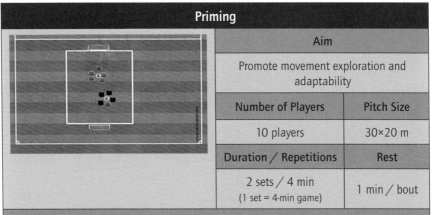

Aim	
Promote movement exploration and adaptability	
Number of Players	**Pitch Size**
10 players	30×20 m
Duration / Repetitions	**Rest**
2 sets / 4 min (1 set = 4-min game)	1 min / bout

Task Description

In this exercise, played as Gk+4vs4+Gk, each team will watch a video that features a specific behavior intended to inspire players during the game. For example, one team may watch a video based on dribbling players (e.g., actions from Cristiano Ronaldo, Messi, Neymar) while the other watches a different video (e.g., players finishing from long distances or playing possession style). The aim of this activity is to inspire players to perform and behave similarly to those featured in the video they watched. Motivational videos may also be used combined with role manipulation (e.g., providing information to one team by stating that they are losing 2-0, and the game has just 10 minutes remaining, while to the other team that they are winning but received an earlier dismissal of two players; in this case, for the first team, it may be shown a video of a team scoring two goals in less than 3 minutes, while showing to the other team a team defending cohesively).

Adding Variability

Combine the videos with material (e.g., emphasizing dribbling while using obstacles or asking for the team to mimic Guardiola's teams by playing possession style using different types of balls, forcing the players to develop new strategies for holding the ball). Use cartoons featuring characters with superpowers to inspire youth players.

Task Material

Markers for the pitch boundaries and areas; 4 bibs; 3 soccer balls; different types of balls

The Superhero	
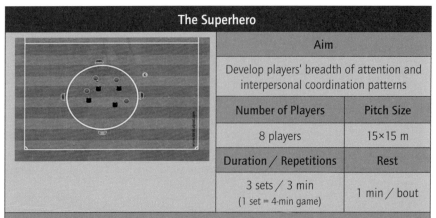	**Aim**
	Develop players' breadth of attention and interpersonal coordination patterns
	Number of Players / **Pitch Size**
	8 players / 15×15 m
	Duration / Repetitions / **Rest**
	3 sets / 3 min (1 set = 4-min game) / 1 min / bout

Task Description

This task is played with four small goals that have smart light inside of them that will change colors at a specific time (e.g., Fitlights, BlazePod), so that at every 10th second, one goal will have a green light that is present for three seconds, and players will attempt to score in that goal during that time. This teaches players to not only perceive the environment but also be able to maintain possession in case they are unable to score in that moment. Other colors may be used to make the task more difficult (e.g., if the team scores in the red colored goal, they will lose one point, or if they score in the yellow-colored goal, they must play at two touches). After scoring a goal, the player will role a dice featuring graphics that will give him "superpowers" (e.g., a flash graphic means that the opposing team can only move with both feet together like a rabbit would, conferring "speed" to the team that scored).

Adding Variability

Instead of using smart lights, three goalkeepers may defend the four goals, increasing the task difficulty.

Task Material

Markers for the pitch boundaries; 4 small goals; 4 smart lights; 4 bibs; 3 soccer balls

Floating Pitch

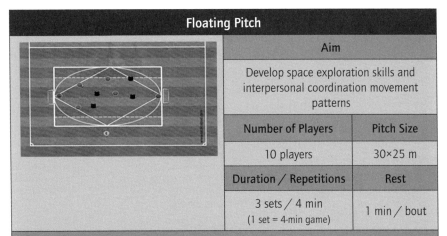

Aim	
Develop space exploration skills and interpersonal coordination movement patterns	
Number of Players	**Pitch Size**
10 players	30×25 m
Duration / Repetitions	**Rest**
3 sets / 4 min (1 set = 4-min game)	1 min / bout

Task Description

This exercise is played as Gk+4vs4+Gk and performed on a pitch that contains different boundaries and configurations. That is, the white lines mark the regular pitch (i.e., rectangular shape pitch, see the figure); the yellow dashed lines represent a narrow pitch (i.e., a pitch with clearly lower width compared to length); a white diamond shape is another pitch; and lastly the yellow lines represent a circular pitch. All pitch boundaries are inside the regular pitch, so the coach can vary the pitch where the players are performing without needing to stop play (e.g., if the players are performing in the regular pitch, the coach can then say diamond pitch, and the players have 2 seconds to adjust their positioning to pitch marked by the yellow lines). Every 20 seconds (or another period of time determined by the coach), the coach will modify the available playing area, exposing the players to different pitch spaces and shapes: (a) regular pitch, (b) small pitch (represented in the image by the yellow dashed lines), (c) diamond pitch, (d) circular pitch. When the coach calls out a new space, the players should move as fast as possible to that space. If the ball leaves its boundaries, the game restarts with a throw-in; however, a small time window (half second) will be provided for the players to adjust and move to the new pitch space.

Adding Variability

Include new types of balls or combine with individual body restrictions. Also, different spaces can be used to challenge the players to perform according to different sports rules (e.g., yellow circle pitch to be played as rugby).

Task Material

6 soccer balls; 4 bibs; markers (of different colors) for pitch boundaries; different types of balls

The Substitute

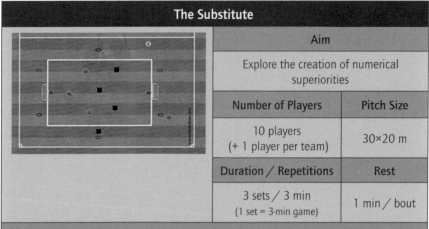

Aim	
Explore the creation of numerical superiorities	
Number of Players	**Pitch Size**
10 players (+ 1 player per team)	30×20 m
Duration / Repetitions	**Rest**
3 sets / 3 min (1 set = 3-min game)	1 min / bout

Task Description

To start, each team has one player outside the pitch in one of the three training rings available. This game is played as Gk+3vs3+Gk plus the 2 extra players (1 per team). When one player passes the ball to a member of his own team (who is outside the pitch), the player who received the ball can travel with it inside the pitch and attempt to score, pass, or dribble (i.e., he joins the game). In turn, the player that passed the ball must move to one of the free training rings.

Adding Variability

Use pitch obstacles to promote player interaction. Promote perceptual constraints (e.g., not using bibs to increase breadth of attention). Rules can be also manipulated (e.g., when the player from outside receives the ball [imagine that he is in the middle training ring], he can decide to which target he will attack).

Task Material

6 training rings; 4 bibs; 2 regular goals; 6 soccer balls; markers for the pitch boundaries

Fourball

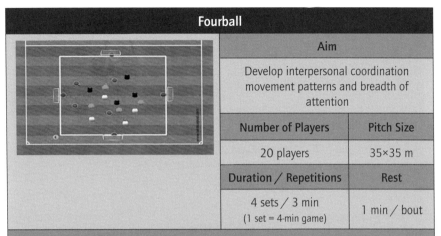

Aim	
Develop interpersonal coordination movement patterns and breadth of attention	
Number of Players	Pitch Size
20 players	35×35 m
Duration / Repetitions	Rest
4 sets / 3 min (1 set = 4-min game)	1 min / bout

Task Description

This exercise involves four teams (Gk+4 players per team), where two teams face each other in the same space while the other two teams are competing against each other in different orientations. To start the game, the coach should define a direction to which both teams must travel (e.g., blue and red attack longitudinally, while green and white laterally). In this case, the variability is imposed by the four teams playing in the same space.

Adding Variability

Instead of having fixed goals, coaches may change the target location of each team by placing one vest of each color in each target that can be changed per time period (e.g., at every 90 seconds, the coach changes the direction of attack for each team). Without stopping the game, promote different team competitions (e.g., red vs blue). If the aim is to increase players' perceptual demands, coaches may also remove the players' bibs, which enhances their need to explore the environment.

Task Material

10 soccer balls; 12 bibs (3 sets of 4 different colors); markers for pitch boundaries

Mini Rugby

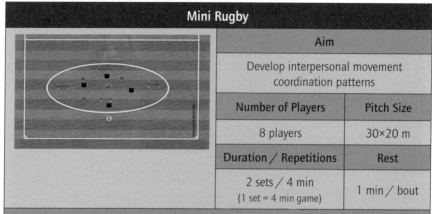

Aim	
Develop interpersonal movement coordination patterns	
Number of Players	**Pitch Size**
8 players	30×20 m
Duration / Repetitions	**Rest**
2 sets / 4 min (1 set = 4 min game)	1 min / bout

Task Description

In this game (4vs4), players use both the hands and feet to score in targets that consist of two agility poles with a rope connecting them in the middle, creating an upper and lower target. At the coach's instruction, goals may be scored below or above the rope and within the agility poles limits (i.e., in height). Also, the coach may include agility poles of different colors to increase perceptual demands (e.g., by defining which target is available or making the players score with different rules according to the color of the target that they are attempting to score in).

Adding Variability

Different balls can be used to expose the players to increased technical complexity. Additionally, coaches may also use cards featuring different types of sports, and the players would be required to play according to whichever sport is featured on the card they've chosen. While the task was designed to have only two teams facing each other, coaches may also create teams (e.g., four teams of three players competing AvsB and CvsD or six teams of two players competing AvsB, CvsD, and EvsF).

Task Material

8 agility poles with 4 ropes;4 bibs; 4 soccer balls; markers for the pitch boundaries; different types of balls

Chameleon

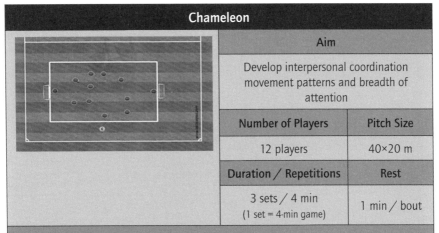

Aim	
Develop interpersonal coordination movement patterns and breadth of attention	
Number of Players	**Pitch Size**
12 players	40×20 m
Duration / Repetitions	**Rest**
3 sets / 4 min (1 set = 4-min game)	1 min / bout

Task Description

In this exercise (Gk+5vs5+Gk), the coach will manipulate the players' bibs according to different possibilities to emphasize the need for them to explore and interact with the environment: (a) both teams playing wearing the same color bib or (b) each player wearing a different colored bib. This is a regular game, where the only variation is in the players' bibs, which affects how the players explore their environments.

Adding Variability

Play with different types of balls. Also, to emphasize the perceptual demands, players may perform the exercise wearing eye patches, or all players can be assigned a different perceptual constraint (e.g., the goalkeeper, instead of wearing regular gloves plays wearing plastic gloves; player one plays barefoot; player two plays wearing a tennis shoe on one foot and nothing on the other foot; player three plays wearing an eye patch; player four plays with their ears covered with a wool cap; player five plays wearing plastic bags on their feet). Alternatively, the coach may put scraps of paper bearing different letters and numbers into a box, and the paper that each player draws determines which two players they are allowed to pass to (e.g., player A can only pass to teammate C and E).

Task Material

10 soccer balls; 20 bibs(10 blue and 10 of different colors, such as 2 white, 2 yellow, 2 red, 2 blue and 2 orange); plastic bags; markers for pitch boundaries; different types of balls

Doublockey

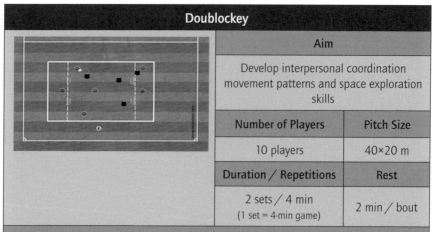

Aim	
Develop interpersonal coordination movement patterns and space exploration skills	
Number of Players	**Pitch Size**
10 players	40×20 m
Duration / Repetitions	**Rest**
2 sets / 4 min (1 set = 4-min game)	2 min / bout

Task Description

This is a hockey-like game (Gk+4vs4+Gk situation) in which each team attempts to score in two small goals defended by a goalkeeper. The goalkeeper area is defined by the white line. There are no restrictions in the space occupied by the players (i.e., players can move freely and must explore the game space, looking for the best way possible to score).

Adding Variability

Vary the location of the goals or allow players to score in all targets (n = four per team). Include training material that would assist the players in achieving success (e.g., having wooden benches or rebounders close to the end line so that the players may use them as a passing option or even to score a goal). These types of obstacles would enhance players' ability to explore unique and different movement solutions (which encourages divergent thinking). In addition, coaches may place one player from each team outside of the pitch, and when he receives the ball, he can travel with it inside while another player (e.g., the player that passed the ball) switches places with him.

Task Material

Different types of balls; 4 small goals; 4 bibs; markers for the pitch boundaries

The List

Aim	
Develop players' movement adaptability and space exploration skills	
Number of Players	**Pitch Size**
10 players	30×20 m
Duration / Repetitions	**Rest**
4 sets / 1 min (1 set = 1-min game)	30 sec / bout

Task Description

In this game (Gk+4vs4+Gk), the pitch is divided into nine zones, and each corresponds to playing with a specific body restriction: (1) hands on the chest, (2) arms in abduction, (3) hands touching the shoulders, (4) hands on the knees, (5) hands holding shorts, (6) right arm behind the head, (7) left arm behind the head, (8) hands tied, or (9) hands touching the heels. When moving between zones, players should change movements. Between bouts, players should change sides so they are exposed to both sides and thus to different training rules.

Adding Variability

Instead of restricting the body, rules such as limiting touches or which part of the foot is allowed to touch the ball can be applied. Also, rules may be applied that prohibit the players to step into specific zones, thereby making them explore different zones. Another option is to apply a rule that specifies that if an opponent receives a ball in a specific zone, that zone may not be occupied by a defensive player (leading the players to create strategies to push the attacking team toward other zones).

Task Material

2 regular goals; 6 soccer balls; 4 bibs;; markers for the pitch boundaries

Two Faces	
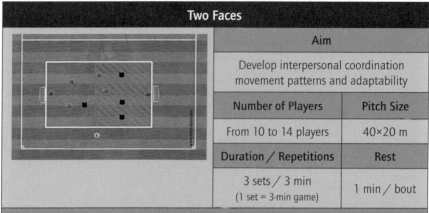	**Aim**
	Develop interpersonal coordination movement patterns and adaptability
	Number of Players	**Pitch Size**
	From 10 to 14 players	40×20 m
	Duration / Repetitions	**Rest**
	3 sets / 3 min (1 set = 3-min game)	1 min / bout

Task Description

This game (Gk+4vs4+Gk) is intended to be played over one pitch with surfaces consisting of a combination of two different types of material, such as artificial turf plus natural grass, artificial turf plus sand, natural grass plus asphalt, or dirt plus artificial turf. The aim is for players to adjust their movement patterns as a result of the space occupied (e.g., the tension applied during a pass would be different if it is performed in the grass or the artificial turf pitch).

Adding Variability

Include different orientations (e.g., left side with natural grass and right side with asphalt). Use pitches with soft declines (similar to a golf pitch or the Malmö Puckelball pitch). To expose players to a certain zone of the pitch for a longer duration of time, the game may also be played in the Korfball mode, where two players per team perform on each side.

Task Material

2 regular goals; 6 soccer balls; 4 bibs; markers for the pitch boundaries

El Rondo		
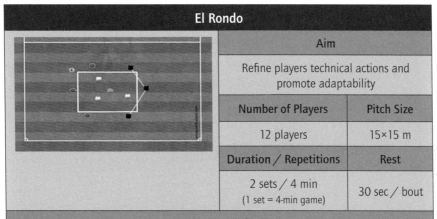	Aim	
	Refine players technical actions and promote adaptability	
	Number of Players	Pitch Size
	12 players	15×15 m
	Duration / Repetitions	Rest
	2 sets / 4 min (1 set = 4-min game)	30 sec / bout

Task Description

This is a rondo (3+3+1vs3) ball possession task based on three teams maintaining ball possession (e.g., blue, white, red) with the help of one neutral (inside) player (green). The red team plays connected by ropes, the blue team with body restrictions (e.g., both hands on the chest, both hands on the back of the head), and the white team under perceptual constraints (e.g., while wearing an eye patch). The green player can also play under varied conditions (e.g., be required to pass in different ways). The team in the middle will change roles when recovering the ball and will perform using the same constraints used by the team that lost the ball.

Adding Variability

Play with different types of balls. Also, rather than having different constraints per team, the coach may define different constraints between the pitch corner (e.g., left side perform with hands on chest, right side play barefoot, upper side play connected, down side play wearing an eye patch). The surface (turf, sand, dirt) and the shape of the pitch (square, diagonal, triangular) may also be modified.

Task Material

2 ropes; 3 eye patches; 7 bibs (3 white, 3 blue, 3 red, 1 green); 6 soccer balls; markers for the pitch boundaries; different types of balls

Guess Where

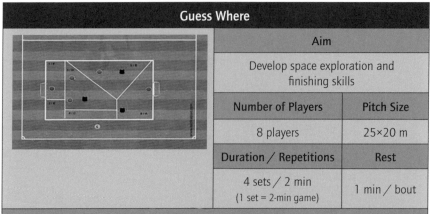

Aim	
Develop space exploration and finishing skills	
Number of Players	**Pitch Size**
8 players	25×20 m
Duration / Repetitions	**Rest**
4 sets / 2 min (1 set = 2-min game)	1 min / bout

Task Description

In this game (Gk+3vs3+Gk), the pitch is divided into zones, from where the players cannot shoot, must shoot, cannot play, or must step in before scoring. These rules may be modified at fixed timestamps (e.g., every 60 seconds) or using varied time windows, such as applying the first rule during the first 30 seconds, the second in the following 15 seconds, and the third in the remaining 25 seconds. The intention is for the offensive players to explore different zones within which to shoot (variation in distance, angles, etc.) while the defensive team tries to protect specific zones to avoid shots. To specify these rules, the coach says, for example, "3 E," meaning that one team can only score from zone three and the other from zone E or that both teams must step in these zones before scoring.

Adding Variability

Attribute to each zone a different way of shooting (e.g., with the head or by raising the ball and shooting in the air). Limit the number of players in certain zones (e.g., zone three can be defended by only one player).

Task Material

2 regular goals; 3 bibs; 6 soccer balls; markers for the pitch boundaries

Wonderland

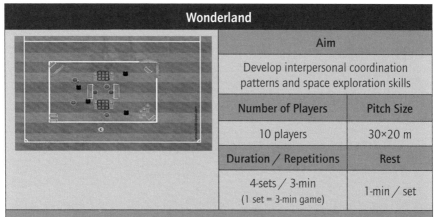

Aim	
Develop interpersonal coordination patterns and space exploration skills	
Number of Players	**Pitch Size**
10 players	30×20 m
Duration / Repetitions	**Rest**
4-sets / 3-min (1 set = 3-min game)	1-min / set

Task Description

In this game (Gk+4vs4+Gk), two teams face each other, and one scores in the two regular goals while the other scores in the four small goals. The regular targets are surrounded by training mannequins and a net to limit movements and shots from specific zones, while the small goals have obstacles (e.g., wooden benches or training mannequins or even two goals close to each other) to make it more difficult to score. After each bout, the coach may change which target is defended by each team. The main intention is for the players to search for novel solutions and ways to shoot at the target and attempt to score.

Adding Variability

Require each team to defend one regular goal and two small goals, perform with different types of balls (e.g., balls with higher bouncing properties), or play under perceptual demands (e.g., while wearing eye patch).

Task Material

2 regular goals; 5 small goals; 4 bibs; 6 soccer balls; 7 training mannequins; 2 nets; 3 wooden benches; markers for boundaries; different types of balls

The Clock	
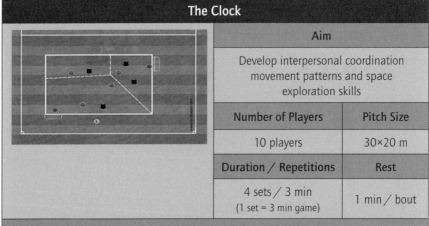	**Aim**
	Develop interpersonal coordination movement patterns and space exploration skills

Number of Players	Pitch Size
10 players	30×20 m

Duration / Repetitions	Rest
4 sets / 3 min (1 set = 3 min game)	1 min / bout

Task Description

This game is played as Gk+4vs4+Gk; the pitch is divided into three different zones, and players are assigned to each. Coaches may use either balanced situations at each zone or create unbalanced scenarios (e.g., zone A, 1vs1; zone B, 2vs1; zone C, 1vs2). The intention is to promote variations in the space occupied (i.e., player A1 and B1 might be playing in zone A from up to 1 minute before joining player B4 in zone C for 2 to 3 minutes). This can be done by moving the players from one team during one bout and then moving the other team's players during the second bout, so they face different opponents or numerical relations every minute.

Adding Variability

Assign different rules to each zone, such as playing with body restrictions (e.g., with hands on chest, with hands tied, with hands holding shorts). Play with different parts of the foot (e.g., non-dominant limb, internal part of the foot, external part of the foot).

Task Material

2 regular goals; 4 bibs; 6 soccer balls; markers for boundaries

Meso-Level Tasks (Collective Level)

Treasure Hunt		
	**Aim**	
	Develop offensive adaptive coordination movement patterns	
	Number of Players	**Pitch Size**
	21 players	30×20 m
	Duration / Repetitions	**Rest**
	6 sets / 2 min (1 set = 2-min game)	30 sec / bout

Task Description
In this game (Gk+10vs10), lines are added on the pitch that will define how the defensive line should be positioned, and the period of play is defined by the coach. Variations should include manipulation in the defensive lines' depth: (a) the defensive sector should play after the first or second line, (b) all players should defend behind the first line, [2] defensive sector in the middle sector and midfielders and forwards in front of the line close to the halfway line. The defensive team, when recovering, may score in one of the small targets. This task aims to develop players' ability to identify space based on the positioning of the opposing team.

Adding Variability
Play under perceptual demands (e.g., without bibs, while wearing eye patches). Rather than manipulate the defensive team's space occupation, modify the offensive team's playing structure (e.g., 4-1-4-1; 3-4-3) to place more focus on the defensive team's behavior.

Task Material
1 regular goal; 3 small goals; 6 soccer balls; 10 bibs; markers for the pitch lines and boundaries

Open the Gates

Aim	
Develop offensive adaptive coordination movement patterns	
Number of Players	**Pitch Size**
16 players	50×64 m
Duration / Repetitions	**Rest**
6 sets / 2 min (1 set = 2-min game)	30 sec / bout

Task Description

This task (Gk+6+NPvs7+NP) is focused on varying the actions of the defensive team. Players from the defensive sector will play tethered to each other in one of the following ways: every two players connected, central defenders connected to midfielders, fullback connected to midfielders, or groups of three players connected. The intention is for the defensive team to adapt according to the rules while the offensive team explores the space that is available as result of the different patterns created by the defensive team. When recovering the ball, the defensive team will be awarded one point by passing the ball to the target player (i.e., green player positioned at the center circle; see figure).

Adding Variability

Instead of tethering together just the defensive players, offensive players may also be tethered together (e.g., right fullback with left winger). Also, specific players (e.g., central defenders) may be assigned to defend using man marking while others are assigned to defend using zones (to enhance space exploration by the attacking team).

Task Material

1 regular goal; 6 soccer balls; 6 bibs; 3 ropes; markers for the pitch lines and boundaries

Good vs. Bad Neighbors

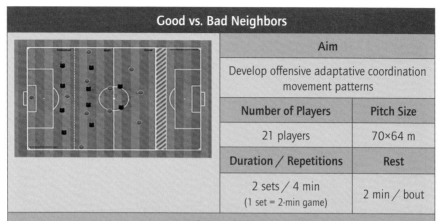

Aim	
Develop offensive adaptative coordination movement patterns	
Number of Players	**Pitch Size**
21 players	70×64 m
Duration / Repetitions	**Rest**
2 sets / 4 min (1 set = 2-min game)	2 min / bout

Task Description

This task (Gk+10vs10) is focused on varying the actions of the defensive team. Accordingly, the pitch is divided into three sectors, and players will have to behave differently based on which sector they are in: (a) offensive sector, zonal pressing, (b) midfield sector, two outside players defend zonal while two central midfielders individual marking (or vice versa), (c) individual marking in the defensive sector (three of the four defenders will individually mark one opposing player). The team in possession should explore different movement solutions to progress and find space as a result of the different types of marking. When recovering the ball, the defensive team is awarded one point if one of their players receives a ball in the white zone.

Adding Variability

Coaches may increase variability by changing the available space (e.g., using narrow or diagonally shaped pitches).

Task Material

1 regular goal; 6 soccer balls; 10 bibs; markers for the pitch boundaries

Social Distance

Aim	
Develop offensive adaptive coordination movement patterns	
Number of Players	**Pitch Size**
21 players	70×64 m
Duration / Repetitions	**Rest**
2 sets / 4 min (1 set = 4-min game)	2 min / bout

Task Description

This task (Gk+10vs10) is focused on varying the actions of the defensive team. Under this perspective, the pitch is divided into four zones, and in each, the defensive team will be assigned a specific behavior that will not be told to the offensive team. As such, the behavior in two zones will be applying high pressure when the ball arrives to the zone, and in the other two zones, the team will focus on delaying and only intercepting passes. This type of task emphasizes space exploration by the offensive team. When recovering the ball, the defensive team has to score two goals without a goalkeeper, so the opposing team is able to press and avoid goal scoring opportunities.

Adding Variability

Vary the type of ball used (e.g., play with balls of lower dimensions). Also, coaches may limit the number of players from each team in specific zones or create spaces where one team can step but not the other, while other zones are available to both teams and others prohibited. Playing without bibs (perceptual demands) or overloading one team (e.g., assigning 14 players to the defensive team) may also be used to promote adaptability and the search for functional behaviors.

Task Material

3 regular goals; 6 soccer balls; 10 bibs; markers for the pitch boundaries; different types of balls

Chasin' You

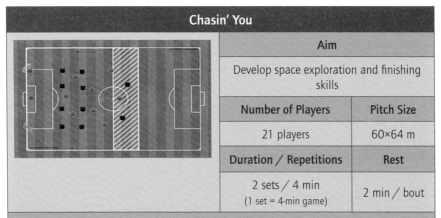

Aim	
Develop space exploration and finishing skills	
Number of Players	**Pitch Size**
21 players	60×64 m
Duration / Repetitions	**Rest**
2 sets / 4 min (1 set = 4-min game)	2 min / bout

Task Description

In this task (Gk+8+2vs10), the coach will vary the number of goals available. For example, (a) all three targets are available, (b) only scoring in diagonal targets is allowed, (c) only scoring in one corridor target is allowed, (d) players must use the central target and score in one of the other two with a specific pattern (e.g., first touch shot). Despite being positioned in this way, at every bout, coaches may also promote adjustments in their angles to emphasize the creation of different goal scoring opportunities and promote more outside or inside playing patterns. The defensive team, when recovering the ball, will attempt to play to the two forwards positioned in the white zone, who can drop down to assist in the attack.

Adding Variability

Due to the high number of shooting possibilities, the defensive team may play with 10+2 players. Use three goals of different sizes (11-a-side; 7-a-side; 5-a-side). Also, offensive players may play with a ball in the hand during the Gk+8+2vs10 to limit their chances of exploring 1vs1 situations and assume more positional play or force each player under possession to touch the ball four times before passing it.

Task Material

3 regular goals; 6 soccer balls; 10 bibs; markers for the pitch boundaries

The Shuttle	
	Aim
	Develop offensive adaptive coordination movement patterns and space exploration skills

Number of Players	Pitch Size
21 players	70×64 m

Duration / Repetitions	Rest
4 sets / 3 min (1 set = 3-min game)	1 min / bout

Task Description

In this game (Gk+10vs10), the playing pitch is varied in one of the following ways to modify the available space for the offensive team: (1) regular pitch (normal lines); (2) narrow pitch (dashed lines); (3) shuttle-like pitch to promote inside movements (yellow lines). The coach may manipulate the pitch boundary lines dynamically (i.e., change the pitch available—such as 1 - regular, 2 - narrow or 3 - shuttle—during a ball possession or after each ball possession). Also, the space can be modified in relation to the team in possession (e.g., if the blue team has the ball, the space is the yellow lines, but if the red team recovers, the space is the white dashed lines).

Adding Variability

Add variability to each sector (e.g., midfielders from both teams playing without bibs; central defenders holding one ball with both hands, fullbacks playing with body restrictions). To increase the cognitive load and search for space, the game can also be played with one attacker holding a football in the hand, and when the ball from the ground is caught, the football is released.

Task Material

2 regular goals; 6 soccer balls; 10 bibs; markers for the pitch boundaries

Roulette

Aim	
Develop players movement adaptability and space exploration skills	
Number of Players	**Pitch Size**
22 players	70×64 m
Duration / Repetitions	**Rest**
4 sets / 4 min (1 set = 4-min game)	1 min / bout

Task Description

This task is played as Gk+10v10+Gk and focuses on exposing the players to perform according to general principles of play, as they will change their playing system at a timespan defined by the coach (e.g., every minute, at every ball possession, every two minutes). The intention is to expose the players from both teams to the same or different playing formations (e.g., 4×4x2 vs 5×4×1; 3×4×3 vs 3×4×3; 4×2×3×1 vs 3×5×2).

Adding Variability

While the teams are facing different playing positions, they might both be exposed to the same playing structure. Also, coaches may promote the use of other types of balls or even remove the bibs to increase the players' focus of attention. Likewise, and depending on the players' expertise, the coach may decide to alter only one team's playing shape so that the other team has to adjust in relation to how the opposing team plays.

Task Material

2 regular goals; 6 soccer balls; 10 bibs; markers for the pitch boundaries; different types of balls

Hot Ball

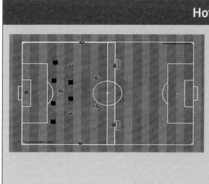

Aim	
Develop offensive technical adaptability and space exploration skills	
Number of Players	**Pitch Size**
16 players	52×64 m
Duration / Repetitions	**Rest**
2 sets / 3 min (1 set = 3-min game)	1 min / bout

Task Description

In this task (Gk+6vx7+2Gk), the offensive team will play with additional body restrictions (e.g., with hands tied) or while holding a ball, to limit the movement by the players in possession (which are also in numerical superiority). When recovering, the defensive team will have two targets to score in. The variability is created by constraining the body movements of the attacking team.

Adding Variability

Use smaller or differently shaped balls. Defenders may also hold tennis balls to limit the possibility of them trying to hold on to the clothes of the attacking players. Instead of playing with a ball in their hands, players may perform on pitches of different surfaces. The space where the defenders can act and defend may also be manipulated (e.g., low block; mid-block; not allowed to defend inside the penalty box).

Task Material

3 regular goals; 12 soccer balls; 10 bibs; markers for the pitch boundaries; different types of balls

Chasing Rules

Aim	
Develop adaptative coordination movement patterns and space exploration skills	
Number of Players	**Pitch Size**
18 players	70×64 m
Duration / Repetitions	**Rest**
4 sets / 4 min (1 set = 4-min game)	1 min / bout

Task Description

In this game (Gk+8vs8+Gk), the pitch is divided into five zones, and in each, a different rule will apply (can be the same for both teams or different between teams) such as (1) free play; (2) one touch; (3) ABC, meaning that player B who received the ball from player A, can pass to all teammates except to the player who passed the ball to him; (4) two touches; (5) three mandatory touches. Alternatively, coaches may specify how many players from each team should cover each zone.

Adding Variability

Instead of assigning specific rules to each zone, every ball possession may result in substitution of one zone for another (e.g., zone three may not be used during the first possession but allowed during the second, while zone two becomes prohibited during this possession). Each zone may also be designed a different playing shape (e.g., zone one, square; zone two, triangle; zone three, circle; zone four, diamond; zone five, 90-degree triangle).

Task Material

2 regular goals; 12 soccer balls; 10 bibs; markers for the pitch boundaries

The Three Kingdoms

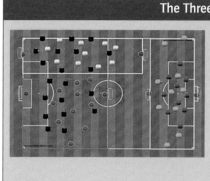

Aim	
Develop interpersonal coordination movement patterns and space exploration skills	
Number of Players	Pitch Size
22 players	Varied
Duration / Repetitions	Rest
3 sets / 3 min (1 set = 3-min game)	1 min / bout

Task Description

This task (Gk+10vs10+Gk) is intended to expose the players to high spatiotemporal pressure as there is little space available in relation to the number of players. In this sense, the coach may vary the pitch boundaries at every bout. There are three pitches: 1) square pitch with goals in one side (allows players from one side to be always close to the goal and perform with less time to decide); 2) narrow pitch (emphasizes the exploration of vertical passes); 3) wide pitch (emphasize the use of the pitch width). Alternatively, the coach may specify a specific number of players in the square pitch (e.g., Gk+6vs6+Gk), while the remaining players can be distributed toward one or the two pitches, and every time a player scores a goal, he will change pitch to create different numbers in the three pitches (e.g., player 5 from blue team scores a goal in pitch one, so he will move and assist the team in pitch two).

Adding Variability

Add perceptual demands (e.g., playing without bibs or using eye patches). Pitches may also be designed with different types of shapes.

Task Material

6 regular goals; 12 soccer balls; 10 bibs; markers for the pitch boundaries

Chasing Players

Aim	
Develop adaptive movement patterns	
Number of Players	**Pitch Size**
14 players	60×64 m
Duration / Repetitions	**Rest**
4 sets / 6 reps (1 rep = 1 attack against defense ball possession)	1 min / bout

Task Description

This task consists of varying the number of players from both teams (offensive and defensive) at each bout (from Gk+1vs1 to Gk+7vs6). To that end, the coach will say two numbers, and the first corresponds to the number of defenders that will participate while the second corresponds to the number of players to attack. For example, 5vs3 means that there will be five defenders and three attackers. To increase task complexity, the coach may add rules such as saying "5vs3 plus two," which means that two additional defenders will join the process. Note that, when possible, the same defender should not be repeated (e.g., if in one set play is defined 4vs3, all four defenders may take part, but if in the following set the number is less than four defenders, it must be the three red players in the center zone of the pitch that defend).

Adding Variability

Perform without bibs to increase perceptual demands or with each player wearing a different vest.

Task Material

1 regular goal; 12 soccer balls; 7 bibs; 6 agility poles; markers for the pitch boundaries

Pay Attention!	
	Aim
	Develop adaptive interpersonal coordination movement patterns and technical adaptability

Number of Players	Pitch Size
18 players	50×35 m

Duration / Repetitions	Rest
3 sets / 4 min (1 set = 4-min game)	2 min / bout

Task Description

This is a 9vs9 large-sided game, where each team is composed of three subunits of three players (3+3+3) wearing the same color (blue and red) but in different shades (e.g., light, medium, and dark blue). The main principle is to create a different rule for each group of three players. For example, light blue can only pass to medium blue, who in turn can only pass to dark blue, who then can only pass to light blue, or light red can only perform at one touch, medium red can only use their nondominant foot, and dark red can only pass the ball without using the foot (e.g., using the knee or head instead).

Adding Variability

Promote the use of dynamic goals (e.g., vary the location or number of goals available) or perform with different types of balls.

Task Material

6 small goals; 18 bibs (9 blue and 9 red); 8 soccer balls; markers for the pitch boundaries

The Shooter

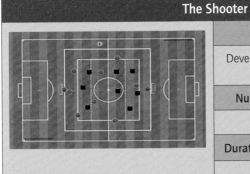

Aim	
Develop players' finishing patterns under different angles and distances	
Number of Players	**Pitch Size**
18 players	Varied
Duration / Repetitions	**Rest**
2 sets / 6 min (1 set = 6-min game)	1 min / bout

Task Description

This task is a Gk+8vs8+Gk game, in which the players will have to adapt their behaviors as result of the following pitch boundaries: (a) regular pitch marked with white lines, representing the large pitch; (b) medium pitch marked with yellow lines that will force the player to shoot farther away from the goal; and (c) a wide pitch marked with white dashed lines that is wider than it is long and has a longer distance to the goal. By varying the respective pitch boundaries, coaches are emphasizing different opportunities to shoot to the target. The variations in each the pitch are based on time (e.g., at every time) or rules (e.g., after every goal).

Adding Variability

The pitch zones may also be different for each team, creating spatial advantage in certain zones, which would require strategy to attain that space, while the defensive team must limit the attacking team's chances to achieve this space. For example, team A might be playing on the regular pitch, while team B is on the wide pitch.

Task Material

2 regular goals; 8 bibs; 8 soccer balls; markers for the pitch boundaries

Under Construction		
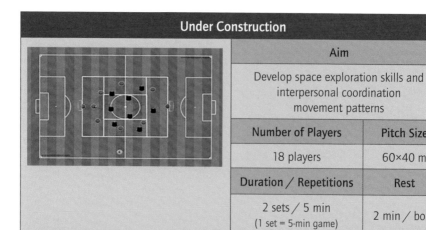	**Aim**	
	Develop space exploration skills and interpersonal coordination movement patterns	
	Number of Players	**Pitch Size**
	18 players	60×40 m
	Duration / Repetitions	**Rest**
	2 sets / 5 min (1 set = 5-min game)	2 min / bout

Task Description

This game (Gk+8vs8+Gk) is played on a pitch divided by zones, where coaches will dynamically allow or restrain spaces where each team can or cannot move. For example, the blue team is allowed to play in all zones except for the central zone, so they should explore adaptive movements to progress down the field (note that players can cross the central zone but not receive the ball there), while the red team cannot play in the last offensive sector and as such should be shooting from a higher distance.

Adding Variability

Instead of restricting or allowing spaces, assign benefits to the different zones (e.g., scoring from one zone would earn the team another ball possession or passing at first touch would mean that the players who performed the pass can receive the ball without offside rule). The rules applied to one team will also affect the other (e.g., if one player has no offside rule, then the defending team may defend closer to their goal to limit the space at their backs).

Task Material

2 regular goals; 8 bibs; 8 soccer balls; markers for the pitch boundaries

Up and Down	
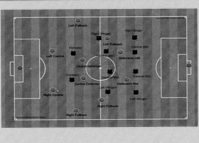	**Aim**
	Develop movement adaptability and space exploration skills

Number of Players	Pitch Size
22 players	104×64 m

Duration / Repetitions	Rest
4 sets / 4 min (1 set = 4-min game)	2 min / bout

Task Description

This exercise consists of a regular 11-a-side game (Gk+10vs10+Gk); however, the intention is to vary the players' playing positions. As such, some different possibilities can be considered: (1) combine the most defensive players into one team, such as the two right fullbacks, two left fullbacks, four central defenders, and two defensive midfielders, while the other team has the four central midfielders, four wingers (two left and two right), and two forwards; (2) vary players' positions, such as having forwards as central defenders, fullbacks as midfielders, or midfielders as fullbacks; (3) combine players from different age groups (e.g., combine five players from U21 with five players from U19).

Adding Variability

Increase the number of players during the task (e.g., have one team with 14 players and another with 12). In addition, coaches may also adopt unusual playing patterns (2-6-2, 6-1-3) to expose players to different spaces to explore.

Task Material

2 regular goals; 10 bibs; 8 soccer balls; markers for the pitch boundaries

CHAPTER 5

Periodization of Variability

Research focused on the periodization of variability is scarce. Otte and collaborators (2019) developed a framework known as the Periodization of Skill Training (PoST) to assist coaches in planning players' skills acquisition and development and to support the structure of the previous categories of tasks. The first stage of this framework is "coordinative training," which focuses on the search and exploration of movement patterns. The training tasks should thus encompass more elementary levels of task complexity and environmental variability (Otte et al., 2019; Otte et al., 2020).

For that purpose, coaches may adjust the level of the task using variable equipment but without dynamic variability (where at every repetition a new movement pattern is required). Therefore, while performing tasks that involve traveling with the ball, coaches may use heavier balls with younger players to allow them to stay on the ball for a longer period, which involves varying the regular equipment (e.g., size 3 soccer ball) to a heavier ball. The next stage is "skill adaptability training," which focuses on promoting movement adaptability by including noise and variability during the training tasks. This stage encompasses three levels: (1) movement variability, (2) complex training, and (3) team-based training. In the first level (movement variability), the focus is on increasing the movement variability at an individual level so that players develop an ability to adapt their movement pattern according to changes in the environment (Otte et al., 2019; Otte et al., 2020). This variability can be added with differential learning and applied in the nanoscale of analysis (that is, situations where the player will train under more analytical scenarios [without opposition] or during the micro-scale of analysis where the player may compete against one opponent [e.g., 1vs1 using different types of balls] under more realistic game scenarios). The second level (complex training) involves recreating environments with a small group of players (Otte et al., 2019;

Otte et al., 2020), such as those found during the meso-scale of analysis (e.g., playing a Gk+4vs4+Gk in a pitch where the boundaries will be changed each minute). Last, the third level (team-based training) consists of a more collective-based task (Otte et al., 2019; Otte et al., 2020) (i.e., using all the team or larger groups, such as those found in the macro-scale) with additional variability (e.g., varying the defensive shape every two minutes between 4x4x2, 4x1x4x1, and 4x2x3x1 to enhance the search for space by the offensive team and adaptive behaviors by the defensive team in terms of distances and space covered between them). The last stage in the PoST framework from Otte and collaborators (2019) is performance training, which is designed to increase players' focus on the environment for maximum performance with lower levels of variability (e.g., using one team to behave in the same way as the opposing team to enhance team readiness for the game).

The aim is to create suitable environments to achieve the intended learning while maintaining the flexibility to adapt to the challenges of the environment.

The PoST framework provides a general overview of how to adjust the level of variability according to the players' level of skill acquisition. To further assist coaches in applying the design task with additional variability, we have developed an example of a training microcycle (European model) with the level of variability per day and with examples of training tasks (see figure 6). Accordingly, the first session (matchday plus 1: MD+1) is typically focused on recovery for the players who played during the game, while the non-used players and substitutes ordinarily have a load day.

Based on that assumption, we propose some general training exercises (low level of variability) for the players who are recovering, such as playing golf using different balls or playing moonball, which is a game similar to Monopoly board game, where players throw a die and perform a technical challenge corresponding to the number thrown. Both tasks consist of low-intensity activities with additional variability and can be used for team collaboration as well. For players who have a loading session, coaches can use a task where the number of players varies, such as in the "In and Out" game (1vs1 to 4vs4) or the "Abracadabra" game, where the available targets to score change constantly. These tasks allow coaches to provide a game-based stimulus with additional variability. During the strength day (MD-4), which is traditionally focused on accelerations, decelerations, and changes-of-direction, we selected tasks that require these types of movements, such as the "Wrestling game," where the players have to stay on the ball for a specific period under pressure from an opponent, or the "Substitute" game, where every time a player from one team goes out, another teammate strategically placed outside of the pitch can move inside. The third session focuses on endurance tasks (MD-3), so tasks such as "The Three Kingdoms" (playing on varied pitch types: narrow, wide, or quarter pitch) or "Treasure Hunt" (where the defending team varies their playing formation in every period) can be used to enhance players' ability to interact with the environmental information and adjust the way the team attacks according to the available space. During the loading days (MD-4, strength day, and MD-3, endurance day), a high level of variability can be added from more micro- to meso-scales (MD-4) and to macro levels (MD-3).

These sessions are the furthest away from the previous and following matches, allowing coaches to explore the players' movement variability. The MD-2 (speed day) is often characterized by training tasks with an emphasis on sprinting and high recovery time. Therefore, more nano and micro tasks were selected for this day, such as the "Sprinter," where players perform sprints under different body restrictions, and "Find a Home," where players have to react to a teammate stimulus and travel with different types of balls toward distinct markers. In the tapering days (MD-2, speed day, and MD-1, activation day), the level of variability can change from low to none to decrease the cognitive load and ensure that players are capable of successfully coping with the tasks to increase their levels of confidence and self-esteem. Note that not all of the tasks must contain variability. The scientific evidence section presents the results

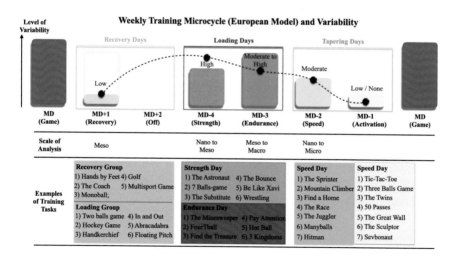

Figure 6. Example of a European training microcycle model and the level of variability to include each day.

from training interventions based on 20 to 30 minutes performed two to three times per week with evident benefits. As such, coaches may decide to include variability during all the sessions in specific tasks or even during the beginning of the sessions.

"A good teacher can never be fixed in a routine. Each moment requires a sensitive mind that is constantly changing and constantly adapting. A teacher must never impose his student to fit his favorite pattern. A good teacher protects his pupils from his own influence. A teacher is never a giver of truth: he is a guide, a pointer to the truth that each student must find for himself. I am not teaching you anything. I just help you to explore yourself."

–Bruce Lee

Concluding Remarks

This book contains a practical approach on how to add variability to soccer training practices. Based on a brief theoretical background and supported by scientific evidence, this book provides a deeper understanding of how variability can aid soccer players' performance. Further, 90 training tasks from different aims and levels of analysis were presented and explained to assist coaches in the design of their own training practices. In fact, the particular aim of this book was not to provide specific exercises but rather to demonstrate examples that may guide coaches to design their own training practices. It is important to note that not all training tasks must encompass the amount of variability presented in the book, as it was developed with the specific focus of emphasizing variability. From this perspective, several examples provided herein, such as using different types of balls and pitches with obstacles and playing with body restrictions and eye patches, were used to highlight the role of variability.

Nevertheless, soccer coaches may increase variability in their practices by introducing simple variations, such as varying the number of players on a task in a dynamic way (e.g., every two minutes) or even the pitch size or space available. With this, we highlight that the game already presents a considerable amount of unpredictability that players will overcome more easily if they are used to continuously overcoming game problems and adapting their behavior as a result of the variations introduced by the coach during the training session.

We believe that adding variability will promote players' potential, as they are challenged to solve their problems, explore different and creative movement solutions, and increase their motor repertoire. Also, the tasks performed with additional variability will create challenging environments that prepare the players to deal with highly complex scenarios, which are likely to increase their performance in competitive settings.

In the long history of humankind (and animalkind, too), those who learned to collaborate and improvise most effectively have prevailed.

Bibliography

Aguiar, Goncalves, Botelho, Lemmink, & Sampaio. (2015). Footballers' movement behaviour during 2-, 3-, 4- and 5-a-side small-sided games. *Journal of Sports Science, 33*(12), 1259-1266. https://doi.org/10.1080/02640414.2015.1022571

Alfonso-Benlliure, Meléndez, & García-Ballesteros. (2013, 2013/12/01/). Evaluation of a creativity intervention program for preschoolers. *Thinking Skills and Creativity, 10*, 112-120. https://doi.org/https://doi.org/10.1016/j.tsc.2013.07.005

Araujo, & Davids. (2016). Team Synergies in Sport: Theory and Measures. *Frontiers in psychology, 7*, 1449. https://doi.org/10.3389/fpsyg.2016.01449

Araújo, Davids, & Hristovski. (2006, Nov). The ecological dynamics of decision making in sport. *Psychology of Sport and Exercise, 7*(6), 653-676. https://doi.org/10.1016/j.psychsport.2006.07.002

Barbado Murillo, Caballero Sánchez, Moreside, Vera-García, & Moreno. (2017, Mar). Can the structure of motor variability predict learning rate? *Journal of Experimental Psychology: Human Perception and Performance, 43*(3), 596-607. https://doi.org/10.1037/xhp0000303

Becker. (1995, 1995/07/01). Nineteenth-Century Foundations of Creativity Research. *Creativity Research Journal, 8*(3), 219-229. https://doi.org/10.1207/s15326934crj0803_2

Becker. (2011). Creativity through history. In M. Runco & S. Pritzker (Eds.), *Encyclopedia of Creativity* (Vol. 1, pp. 303-310). CA: Academic Press.

Bernshteĭn. (1967). *The Co-ordination and Regulation of Movements*. Pergamon Press. https://books.google.pt/books?id=kX5OAQAAIAAJ

Berry, Abernethy, & Côté. (2008, Dec). The contribution of structured activity and deliberate play to the development of expert perceptual and decision-making skill. *Journal of Sport and Exercise Psychology, 30*(6), 685-708. https://doi.org/10.1123/jsep.30.6.685

Boden. (1996). *Dimensions of Creativity*. MIT Press. https://books.google.pt/books?id=xo4CJ6bjid0C

Bowers, Green, Hemme, & Chalip. (2014, 2014/07/01). Assessing the Relationship Between Youth Sport Participation Settings and Creativity in Adulthood. *Creativity Research Journal, 26*(3), 314-327. https://doi.org/10.1080/10400 419.2014.929420

Bozkurt. (2018, 04/23). The Effects of Differential Learning and Traditional Learning Trainings on Technical Development of Football Players. *Journal of Education and Training Studies, 6*, 25. https://doi.org/10.11114/jets.v6i4a.3229

Buszard, Reid, Krause, Kovalchik, & Farrow. (2017). Quantifying Contextual Interference and Its Effect on Skill Transfer in Skilled Youth Tennis Players. *Frontiers in psychology, 8*, 1931. https://doi.org/10.3389/fpsyg.2017.01931

Caballero, Barbado, & Moreno. (2014, 06/30). Non-linear tools and methodological concerns measuring human movement variability: an overview. *European Journal of Human Movement, 32*, 61-81.

Caso, & van der Kamp. (2020, 2020/05/01/). Variability and creativity in small-sided conditioned games among elite soccer players. *Psychology of Sport and Exercise, 48*, 101645. https://doi.org/https://doi.org/10.1016/j.psychsport.2019.101645

Chow, Davids, Button, & Renshaw. (2015). *Nonlinear Pedagogy in Skill Acquisition: An Introduction.* Taylor & Francis. https://books.google.pt/books?id=8N80CwAAQBAJ

Claxton, Pannells, & Rhoads. (2005, 2005/10/01). Developmental Trends in the Creativity of School-Age Children. *Creativity Research Journal, 17*(4), 327-335. https://doi.org/10.1207/s15326934crj1704_4

Côté. (1999). The influence of the family in the development of talent in sport. *The Sport Psychologist, 13*(4), 395-417.

Côté, & Abernethy. (2012). A developmental approach to sport expertise. In S. Murphy (Ed.), *The Oxford Handbook of Sport and Performance Psychology* (pp. 435–447).

Coutinho, Goncalves, Santos, Travassos, Wong, & Sampaio. (2019, Jul-Sep). Effects of the pitch configuration design on players' physical performance and movement behaviour during soccer small-sided games. *Research in Sports Medicine, 27*(3), 298-313. https://doi.org/10.1080/15438627.2018.1544133

Coutinho, Gonçalves, Travassos, Folgado, Figueira, & Sampaio. (2020, 2020/01/02). Different Marks in the Pitch Constraint Youth Players' Performances During Football Small-sided Games. *Research Quarterly for Exercise and Sport, 91*(1), 15-23. https://doi.org/10.1080/02701367.2019.1645938

Coutinho, Santos, Gonçalves, Travassos, Wong, Schöllhorn, & Sampaio. (2018). The effects of an enrichment training program for youth football attackers. *PLoS One, 13*(6), e0199008. https://doi.org/10.1371/journal.pone.0199008

Cropley. (2006, 2006/07/01). In Praise of Convergent Thinking. *Creativity Research Journal, 18*(3), 391-404. https://doi.org/10.1207/s15326934crj1803_13

Davids. (2014). Athletes and sports teams as complex adaptive system: A review of implications for learning design. *RICYDE: Revista Internacional de Ciencias del Deporte, 11*(39), 48-61.

Davids, Button, & Bennett. (2008). *Dynamics of Skill Acquisition: A Constraints-led Approach.* Human Kinetics. https://books.google.pt/books?id=0N-ffZNdEUMC

Davids, Glazier, Araujo, & Bartlett. (2003). Movement systems as dynamical systems - The functional role of variability and its implications for sports medicine. *Sports Medicine, 33*(4), 245-260. https://doi.org/10.2165/00007256-200333040-00001

Duarte, Araujo, Correia, Davids, Marques, & Richardson. (2013, Aug). Competing together: Assessing the dynamics of team-team and player-team synchrony in professional association football. *Human Movement Science, 32*(4), 555-566. https://doi.org/10.1016/j.humov.2013.01.011

Duarte, Araujo, Davids, Travassos, Gazimba, & Sampaio. (2012, May). Interpersonal coordination tendencies shape 1-vs-1 sub-phase performance outcomes in youth soccer. *Journal of Sports Sciences, 30*(9), 871-877. https://doi.org/10.1080/02640414.2012.675081

Fajen. (2005). Perceiving possibilities for action: on the necessity of calibration and perceptual learning for the visual guidance of action. *Perception, 34*(6), 717-740. https://doi.org/10.1068/p5405

Fajen. (2007, 2007/09/21). Affordance-Based Control of Visually Guided Action. *Ecological psychology, 19*(4), 383-410. https://doi.org/10.1080/10407410701557877

Fajen, Riley, & Turvey. (2009). Information, Affordances, and the Control of Action in Sport. *International Journal of Sport Psychology*(40), 79-107. http://panda.cogsci.rpi.edu/resources/papers/FajenRileyTurvey2009.pdf

Farrow, & Robertson. (2017, Jun). Development of a Skill Acquisition Periodisation Framework for High-Performance Sport. *Sports Medicine, 47*(6), 1043-1054. https://doi.org/10.1007/s40279-016-0646-2

Folgado, Bravo, Pereira, & Sampaio. (2019, 2019/05/03). Towards the use of multidimensional performance indicators in football small-sided games: the effects of pitch orientation. *Journal of Sports Sciences, 37*(9), 1064-1071. https://doi.org/10.1080/02640414.2018.1543834

Folgado, Duarte, Fernandes, & Sampaio. (2014). Competing with lower level opponents decreases intra-team movement synchronization and time-motion demands during pre-season soccer matches. *PLoS One, 9*(5), e97145. https://doi.org/10.1371/journal.pone.0097145

Folgado, Gonçalves, & Sampaio. (2017). Positional synchronization affects physical and physiological responses to preseason in professional football (soccer). *Research in sports medicine (Print)*, 1-13. https://doi.org/10.1080/15438627.2017.1393754

Frank, Michelbrink, Beckmann, & Schöllhorn. (2008, Jan). A quantitative dynamical systems approach to differential learning: Self-organization principle and order parameter equations. *Biological Cybernetics, 98*(1), 19-31. https://doi.org/10.1007/s00422-007-0193-x

Gaspar, Santos, Coutinho, Gonçalves, Sampaio, & Leite. (2019). Acute effects of differential learning on football kicking performance and in countermovement jump. *PLoS One, 14*(10), e0224280. https://doi.org/10.1371/journal.pone.0224280

Gibson. (1986). *The Ecological Approach to Visual Perception*. Lawrence Erlbaum Associates. https://books.google.pt/books?id=DrhCCWmJpWUC

Glazier, & Davids. (2009). Constraints on the complete optimization of human motion. *Sports Medicine, 39*(1), 15-28. https://doi.org/10.2165/00007256-200939010-00002

Gonçalves, Coutinho, Exel, Travassos, Lago, & Sampaio. (2019). Extracting spatial-temporal features that describe a team match demands when considering the effects of the quality of opposition in elite football. *PLoS One, 14*(8), e0221368. https://doi.org/10.1371/journal.pone.0221368

Gonçalves, Figueira, Maçãs, & Sampaio. (2014, 2014/01/20). Effect of player position on movement behaviour, physical and physiological performances during an 11-a-side football game. *Journal of Sports Sciences, 32*(2), 191-199. https://doi.org/10.1080/02640414.2013.816761

Gonçalves, Marcelino, Torres-Ronda, Torrents, & Sampaio. (2016, Jul). Effects of emphasising opposition and cooperation on collective movement behaviour during football small-sided games. *Journal of Sports Sciences, 34*(14), 1346-1354. https://doi.org/10.1080/02640414.2016.1143111

Grehaigne, Bouthier, & David. (1997, 1997/01/01). Dynamic-system analysis of opponent relationships in collective actions in soccer. *Journal of Sports Sciences, 15*(2), 137-149. https://doi.org/10.1080/026404197367416

Guilford. (1950). Creativity. *American Psychologist, 5*(9), 444-454. https://doi.org/10.1037/h0063487

Guilford. (1967). *The nature of human intelligence*. McGraw-Hill. https://books.google.pt/books?id=T-ZJAAAAMAAJ

Harrington. (2011). Creative environments, conditions and settings. In M. Runco & S. Pritzker (Eds.), *Encyclopedia of Creativity* (Vol. 1, pp. 264-272). CA: Academic Press.

Henz, & Schöllhorn. (2016). Differential Training Facilitates Early Consolidation in Motor Learning. *Frontiers in Behavioral Neuroscience, 10*. https://doi.org/10.3389/fnbeh.2016.00199

Herzfeld, & Shadmehr. (2014). Motor variability is not noise, but grist for the learning mill. *nature neuroscience, 17*(2), 149-150. https://doi.org/10.1038/nn.3633

Hossner, Käch, & Enz. (2016, 2016/06/01/). On the optimal degree of fluctuations in practice for motor learning. *Human Movement Science, 47*, 231-239. https://doi.org/https://doi.org/10.1016/j.humov.2015.06.007

Hristovski, Davids, Araujo, & Passos. (2011, Apr). Constraints-induced emergence of functional novelty in complex neurobiological systems: A basis for creativity in sport. *Nonlinear Dynamics Psychology and Life Sciences, 15*(2), 175-206.

Kaufman, & Baer. (2012, 2012/01/01). Beyond New and Appropriate: Who Decides What Is Creative? *Creativity Research Journal, 24*(1), 83-91. https://doi.org/10.1080/10400419.2012.649237

Kim. (2006, 2006/01/01). Can We Trust Creativity Tests? A Review of the Torrance Tests of Creative Thinking (TTCT). *Creativity Research Journal, 18*(1), 3-14. https://doi.org/10.1207/s15326934crj1801_2

Komar, Seifert, & Thouvarecq. (2015). What variability tells us about motor expertise: measurements and perspectives from a complex system approach. *Movement & Sport Sciences, 89*(3), 65-77. https://doi.org/10.3917/sm.089.0065

Laakso, Travassos, Liukkonen, & Davids. (2017, Aug). Field location and player roles as constraints on emergent 1-vs-1 interpersonal patterns of play in football. *Human Movement Science, 54*, 347-353. https://doi.org/10.1016/j.humov.2017.06.008

Le Runigo, Benguigui, & Bardy. (2005, Jun). Perception-action coupling and expertise in interceptive actions. *Hum Mov Sci, 24*(3), 429-445. https://doi.org/10.1016/j.humov.2005.06.008

McGarry, Anderson, Wallace, Hughes, & Franks. (2002, Oct). Sport competition as a dynamical self-organizing system. *Journal of Sports Sciences, 20*(10), 771-781. https://doi.org/10.1080/026404102320675620

Memmert. (2006, 2006/06/01). Developing creative thinking in a gifted sport enrichment program and the crucial role of attention processes. *High Ability Studies, 17*(1), 101-115. https://doi.org/10.1080/13598130600947176

Memmert. (2015a). Development of tactical creativity in sports. In K. Baker & D. Farrow (Eds.), *Routledge Handbook of Sport Expertise* (pp. 363-372). Routledge.

Memmert. (2015b). *Teaching Tactical Creativity in Sport: Research and Practice.* Taylor & Francis. https://books.google.pt/books?id=8qIGCAAAQBAJ

Memmert, Baker, & Bertsch. (2010, 2010/06/01). Play and practice in the development of sport-specific creativity in team ball sports. *High Ability Studies, 21*(1), 3-18. https://doi.org/10.1080/13598139.2010.488083

Memmert, & Roth. (2007, Oct). The effects of non-specific and specific concepts on tactical creativity in team ball sports. *Journal of Sports Sciences, 25*(12), 1423-1432. https://doi.org/10.1080/02640410601129755

Newell. (1986a). Constraints on the development of coordination. *Springer*, 341-360. https://doi.org/10.1007/978-94-009-4460-2_19

Newell. (1986b). Constraints on the development of coordination. In M. Wade & H. Whiting (Eds.), *Motor Development in Children: Aspects of Coordination and Control* (pp. 341-360). Springer. https://doi.org/10.1007/978-94-009-4460-2_19

Newell. (1998). The Nature of movement variability. In J. P. Piek (Ed.), *Motor Behavior and Human Skill: A multidisciplinary approach* (pp. 143-160). Human Kinetics.

Newell, Liu, & Mayer-Kress. (2003, 2003/12/01/). A dynamical systems interpretation of epigenetic landscapes for infant motor development. *Infant Behavior and Development, 26*(4), 449-472. https://doi.org/https://doi.org/10.1016/j.infbeh.2003.08.003

Orth, Van Der Kamp, Memmert, & Savelsbergh. (2017). Creative Motor Actions As Emerging from Movement Variability. *Frontiers in psychology, 8*, 1903. https://doi.org/10.3389/fpsyg.2017.01903

Otte, Davids, Millar, & Klatt. (2020, 2020/08/01). Specialist role coaching and skill training periodisation: A football goalkeeping case study. *International Journal of Sports Science & Coaching, 15*(4), 562-575. https://doi.org/10.1177/1747954120922548

Otte, Millar, & Klatt. (2019, 2019-November-15). Skill Training Periodization in "Specialist" Sports Coaching—An Introduction of the "PoST" Framework for Skill Development [Conceptual Analysis]. *Frontiers in Sports and Active Living, 1*(61). https://doi.org/10.3389/fspor.2019.00061

Ozuak, & Çağlayan. (2019, 05/10). Differential Learning as an Important Factor in Training of Football Technical Skills. *Journal of Education and Training Studies, 7*, 68. https://doi.org/10.11114/jets.v7i6.4135

Pabel, Freitag, Hrasky, Zapf, & Wiegand. (2018, Jul). Randomised controlled trial on differential learning of toothbrushing in 6- to 9-year-old children. *Clinical Oral Investigations, 22*(6), 2219-2228. https://doi.org/10.1007/s00784-017-2313-x

Passos, Araujo, & Davids. (2016). Competitiveness and the Process of Co-adaptation in Team Sport Performance. *Front Psychol, 7*, 1562. https://doi.org/10.3389/fpsyg.2016.01562

Pellegrini, Dupuis, & Smith. (2007, 2007/06/01/). Play in evolution and development. *Developmental Review, 27*(2), 261-276. https://doi.org/https://doi.org/10.1016/j.dr.2006.09.001

Pesce, Croce, Ben-Soussan, Vazou, McCullick, Tomporowski, & Horvat. (2019, 2019/03/04). Variability of practice as an interface between motor and cognitive development. *International Journal of Sport and Exercise Psychology, 17*(2), 133-152. https://doi.org/10.1080/1612197X.2016.1223421

Pinder, Davids, Renshaw, & Araujo. (2011, Feb). Representative learning design and functionality of research and practice in sport. *Journal of Sport and Exercise Psychology, 33*(1), 146-155.

Rasmussen, Glīveanu, & Østergaard. (2020). "The principles are good, but they need to be integrated in the right way": Experimenting with creativity in elite youth soccer. *Journal of Applied Sport Psychology*, 1-23. https://doi.org/10.1080/10413200.2020.1778135

Rasmussen, & Østergaard. (2016, 2016/09/01). The Creative Soccer Platform: New Strategies for Stimulating Creativity in Organized Youth Soccer Practice. *Journal of Physical Education, Recreation & Dance, 87*(7), 9-19. https://doi.org/10.108 0/07303084.2016.1202799

Razumnikova. (2007, Jun 15). Creativity related cortex activity in the remote associates task. *Brain Research Bulletin, 73*(1-3), 96-102. https://doi. org/10.1016/j.brainresbull.2007.02.008

Renshaw, Chow, Davids, & Hammond. (2010). A constraints-led perspective to understanding skill acquisition and game play: A basis for integration of motor learning theory and physical education praxis? *Physical Education and Sport Pedagogy, 15*(2), 117-137. https://doi.org/10.1080/17408980902791586

Renshaw, Davids, Newcombe, & Roberts. (2019). *The Constraints-Led Approach (Routledge Studies in Constraints-Based Methodologies in Sport)* (1st Edn ed.). Routledge. https://doi.org/10.4324/9781315102351-6

Richard, Lebeau, Becker, Boiangin, & Tenenbaum. (2018, 2018/10/02). Developing Cognitive and Motor Creativity in Children Through an Exercise Program Using Nonlinear Pedagogy Principles. *Creativity Research Journal, 30*(4), 391-401. https://doi.org/10.1080/10400419.2018.1530913

Runco. (2014). *Creativity: Theories and Themes: Research, Development, and Practice.* Elsevier Science. https://books.google.pt/books?id=XwjUAgAAQBAJ

Runco, & Acar. (2012, 2012/01/01). Divergent Thinking as an Indicator of Creative Potential. *Creativity Research Journal, 24*(1), 66-75. https://doi.org/10.1080/ 10400419.2012.652929

Runco, & Jaeger. (2012, 2012/01/01). The Standard Definition of Creativity. *Creativity Research Journal, 24*(1), 92-96. https://doi.org/10.1080/1040041 9.2012.650092

Sampaio, Gonçalves, Coutinho, Santos, Folgado, & Travassos. (2019). Using tracking data from matches and training situations. In A. Ric & R. Peláez (Eds.), *Football Analytics: Now and Beyond* (pp. 112-131). FC Barcelona.

Santos, Coutinho, Gonçalves, Abade, Pasquarelli, & Sampaio. (2020a). Effects of manipulating ball type on youth footballers' performance during small-sided games. *International Journal of Sports Science & Coaching, 15*(2), 170-183. https://doi.org/10.1177/1747954120908003

Santos, Coutinho, Gonçalves, Schöllhorn, Sampaio, & Leite. (2018, 2018/01/02). Differential Learning as a Key Training Approach to Improve Creative and Tactical Behavior in Soccer. *Research Quarterly for Exercise and Sport, 89*(1), 11-24. https://doi.org/10.1080/02701367.2017.1412063

Santos, Jiménez, Sampaio, & Leite. (2017). Effects of the Skills4Genius sports-based training program in creative behavior. *PLoS One, 12*(2). https://doi.org/10.1371/journal.pone.0172520

Santos, Memmert, Sampaio, & Leite. (2016). The Spawns of Creative Behavior in Team Sports: A Creativity Developmental Framework. *Front Psychol, 7*, 1282. https://doi.org/10.3389/fpsyg.2016.01282

Santos, & Monteiro. (2020). Uncovering the Role of Motor Performance and Creative Thinking on Sports Creativity in Primary School-aged Children. *Creativity Research Journal*, 1-15. https://doi.org/10.1080/10400419.2020.1843125

Santos, Sampaio, & Memmert. (2020b). Sports as a Key Route to Ignite Creativity. In S. Kreitler (Ed.), *New Frontiers in Creativity*. Nova Science Publishers.

Schöllhorn, Hegen, & Davids. (2012). The nonlinear nature of learning - A differential learning approach. *The Open Sports Sciences Journal, 5*, 100–112.

Schöllhorn, & Horst. (2019). Effects of complex movements on the brain as a result of increased decision-making. *Journal of Complexity in Health Sciences, 2*(2), 40-45. https://doi.org/10.21595/chs.2019.21190

Schollhorn, Mayer-Kress, Newell, & Michelbrink. (2009, Jun). Time scales of adaptive behavior and motor learning in the presence of stochastic perturbations. *Human Movement Science, 28*(3), 319-333. https://doi.org/10.1016/j.humov.2008.10.005

Schöllhorn, Michelbrink, Beckmann, Sechelmann, Trockel, & Davids. (2006). Does noise provide a basis for the unification of motor learning theories? *International Journal of Sport Psychology, 37*(2).

Schöllhorn, Michelbrink, Welminsiki, & Davids. (2009). Increasing stochastic perturbations enhances acquisition and learning of complex sport movements. In D. Araujo, Ripoll, Hubert, & Raab, Markus (Ed.), *Perspectives on Cognition and Action in Sport* (pp. 59 -73). Nova Science Publishers, Inc.

Seifert, Button, & Davids. (2013). Key properties of expert movement systems in sport: An ecological dynamics perspective. *Sports Medicine, 43*(3), 167-178. https://doi.org/10.1007/s40279-012-0011-z

Shmuelof, Krakauer, & Mazzoni. (2012, Jul). How is a motor skill learned? Change and invariance at the levels of task success and trajectory control. *Journal of Neurophysiology, 108*(2), 578-594. https://doi.org/10.1152/jn.00856.2011

Stergiou, & Decker. (2011, Oct). Human movement variability, nonlinear dynamics, and pathology: is there a connection? *Human Movement Science, 30*(5), 869-888. https://doi.org/10.1016/j.humov.2011.06.002

Stergiou, Harbourne, & Cavanaugh. (2006). Optimal Movement Variability: A New Theoretical Perspective for Neurologic Physical Therapy. *Journal of Neurologic Physical Therapy, 30*(3). https://journals.lww.com/jnpt/Fulltext/2006/09000/Optimal_Movement_Variability__A_New_Theoretical.6.aspx

Stergiou, Yu, & Kyvelidou. (2013). A Perspective on Human Movement Variability With Applications in Infancy Motor Development. *Kinesiology Review, 2*(1), 93. https://doi.org/10.1123/krj.2.1.93

Sternberg, & Lubart. (1995). *Defying the Crowd: Cultivating Creativity in a Culture of Conformity*. Free Press. https://books.google.pt/books?id=8tp9AAAAMAAJ

Sternberg, & Lubart. (1999). The concept of creativity: Prospects and paradigms. In R. J. Sternberg (Ed.), *Handbook of Creativity* (pp. 3-15). Cambridge University Press.

Travassos, Araujo, Davids, Vilar, Esteves, & Vanda. (2012a, Mar). Informational constraints shape emergent functional behaviours during performance of interceptive actions in team sports. *Psychology of Sport and Exercise, 13*(2), 216-223. https://doi.org/10.1016/j.psychsport.2011.11.009

Travassos, Duarte, Vilar, Davids, & Araujo. (2012b). Practice task design in team sports: representativeness enhanced by increasing opportunities for action. *Journal of Sports Sciences, 30*(13), 1447-1454. https://doi.org/10.1080/02640414.2012.712716

Travassos, Goncalves, Marcelino, Monteiro, & Sampaio. (2014, Dec). How perceiving additional targets modifies teams' tactical behavior during football small-sided games. *Human Movement Science, 38*, 241-250. https://doi.org/10.1016/j.humov.2014.10.005

Tumer, & Brainard. (2007, 12/20/online). Performance variability enables adaptive plasticity of 'crystallized' adult birdsong. *Nature, 450*, 1240.

https://doi.org/10.1038/nature06390;   https://www.nature.com/articles/
nature06390#supplementary-information

Vilar, Araujo, Travassos, & Davids. (2014, Feb). Coordination tendencies are shaped by attacker and defender interactions with the goal and the ball in futsal. *Human Movement Science, 33*, 14-24. https://doi.org/10.1016/j.humov.2013.08.012

Wu, Miyamoto, Castro, Ölveczky, & Smith. (2014, 01/12/online). Temporal structure of motor variability is dynamically regulated and predicts motor learning ability [Article]. *Nature Neuroscience, 17*, 312. https://doi.org/10.1038/nn.3616; https://www.nature.com/articles/nn.3616#supplementary-information

About the Authors

Diogo Coutinho is an assistant professor at the University of Trás-os-Montes and Alto Douro (UTAD) and at the High Institute of Maia (ISMAI), Portugal. He has published more than 25 ISI indexed manuscripts covering performance analysis and movement variability in soccer. He also holds a position as assistant coach in the Portuguese First and Second divisions.

Sara Santos holds a position as researcher at the University of Trás-os-Montes and Alto Douro (UTAD), Portugal. She is an integrated member of the Research Center in Sports Sciences, Health Sciences and Human Development (CIDESD). Sara is the author of several scientific papers published in national and international journals focused on exploring the influence of enrichment environments to nurture creative behavior in youths. Also, she is the coordinator of the Skills4Genius program, which secured funding by the Calouste Gulbenkian Foundation and was awarded by the Olympic Committee of Portugal.

Jaime Sampaio (@Jaime__Sampaio) holds a position of professor with tenure at the University of Trás-os-Montes and Alto Douro in Portugal, teaching and researching Performance Analysis in Team Sports. He is a pro-rector for infrastructures and scientific projects. Formerly, he was the director for the Research Center for Sports, Health and Human Development (CIDESD, 2013-2021). In the university, he heads the CreativeLab research community and two labs—CreativeLab and SporTech—dealing, respectively, with Performance Analysis in Team Sports and Technological Applications in Sports. His research activity is mainly focused on performance analysis in team sports, having produced several publications in international peer-review journals (h-index 49) and textbooks supported by granted projects.

CHECK OUT THESE LATEST SOCCER BOOKS

Dr. Jay Martin

LESSONS FROM THE BEST COACH

DEVELOP A WINNING TEAM CULTURE

A road map all coaches can use to create an environment that is sustainable over time. In nine lessons, Dr. Martin presents the steps he uses to create a winning team culture.

$16.95 US
ISBN 9781782552635

Rob Ellis

THE SOCCER COACH'S TOOLKIT:

MORE THAN 250 ACTIVITIES TO INSPIRE AND CHALLENGE PLAYERS

Gives soccer coaches more than 250 high-quality activities for all age ranges and playing abilities that can either be used as one-off sessions for player development or as part of a competitive training program.

$28.95
ISBN 9781782552178

MEYER & MEYER SPORT

MEYER & MEYER Sport	Phone	+49 02 41 - 9 58 10 - 13
Von-Coels-Str. 390	Fax	+49 02 41 - 9 58 10 - 10
52080 Aachen	E-Mail	sales@m-m-sports.com
Germany	Website	www.m-m-sports.com

FROM MEYER & MEYER SPORT

Dr. Adam Owen

SOCCER SCIENCE & PERFORMANCE COACHING

DEVELOP AN ELITE COACHING METHODOLOGY WITH APPLIED COACHING SCIENCE

Leaders in fields of applied sport science, sport and exercise conditioning, sport psychology, sport nutrition, and strength and conditioning outline the best soccer coaching and training methods for preparing, performing, and recovering.

$34.95 US
ISBN 9781782552482

Fabian Seeger

THE SOCCER GAMES AND DRILLS COMPENDIUM

350 SMART AND PRACTICAL GAMES TO FORM INTELLIGENT PLAYERS—FOR ALL LEVELS

A top seller, this compilation of realistic drills and games facilitates design and quick implementation of modern soccer training. Specific training exercises and graphics make it an optimal resources for coaches.

$32.00 US
ISBN 9781782551041

All information subject to change. © Adobe Stock

MEYER & MEYER Sport
Von-Coels-Str. 390
52080 Aachen
Germany

Phone   +49 02 41 - 9 58 10 - 13
Fax   +49 02 41 - 9 58 10 - 10
E-Mail   sales@m-m-sports.com
Website www.m-m-sports.com

MEYER
& MEYER
SPORT

Credits

Cover and interior design: Anja Elsen
Layout: DiTech Publishing Services, www.ditechpubs.com
Cover photo: © AdobeStock
Interior figures and photos: All images courtesy of the authors
Managing editor: Elizabeth Evans
Copy editor: Carly O'Connor